POWER PRAYERS

for Good Mornings

450 Prayers
to Start Your Day

BARBOUR
PUBLISHING

Our mission is to inspire the world with the life-changing message of the Bible.

Member of the
Evangelical Christian
Publishers Association

POWER
PRAYERS
for Good Mornings

Introduction

What does prayer mean to you? At the very heart of the matter, prayer is sharing with God. It opens up a line of communication that links children to Father, creation to Creator, saved to Savior. Sounds pretty simple, right?

But the truth is that many of us (even longtime Christians) struggle to pray. Whether it's because of a too-full schedule or a too-hard heart or an insecurity about what to pray, it's a challenge—but a challenge worth meeting head-on!

No matter where you are in your prayer journey, this book is a great place to start. Within these pages, you'll find the encouragement you need to start your day in conversation with God. Then short prayer starters will get you headed in the right direction and give you some specific areas to begin your day. Meditate on the accompanying words of scripture and take full advantage of your prayer time, and soon you'll see the blessings that follow a life that is covered in prayer—daily growing closer to the heart of the one who puts the power in our prayers!

The earnest prayer of a righteous person has great power and produces wonderful results.

JAMES 5:16 NLT

Waiting on the Lord

Wait on the Lord; be of good courage, and He shall strengthen your heart; wait, I say, on the LORD!

PSALM 27:14 NKJV

Dear Lord, as I enter into this quiet time with You, calm my mind, body, and spirit. Take my hand and lead me to Your side. I long to feel Your touch, hear Your voice, and see Your face. Whatever comes to me this day, I know You will be with me, as You are now—within me, above me, beside me. Thank You for strengthening my heart. Thank You for giving me the patience to wait on You.

Forgive and Forget

Their sins and their lawless deeds I will remember no more.

HEBREWS 10:17 NASB

Why can't I forgive and forget, Lord? Please help me forgive the person who injured me the other day. Instill in me Your power, Your grace, and Your mercy. With each breath I take in Your presence, I feel that power growing within me. Thank You, Lord. Now, please give me the means to forget this pain. I don't want to keep bringing it up and picking at the wound. Help me, Lord, as weak as I am, to forgive the offender and forget the pain.

Church Division

When you come together as a church,
I hear that divisions exist among you.

1 CORINTHIANS 11:18 NASB

Lord, how can those who are united in belief be so divided in other areas? Please, God, You know what is causing strife in Your house of prayer. Please soothe it with Your healing balm. Give our leaders and members wisdom. Pour out upon us Your love, and remind us of the love we have for each other. Heal the breach, Lord. I put all these concerns in Your hands. Give me the wisdom to leave them there.

An Attitude of Thankfulness

God, I appreciate the good things You put in my life. I know I take them for granted sometimes, and I don't mean to be that way. I get caught up with the fast-paced busyness of all the things I have to do. I need to remember the simple things that bring me joy: a moment of laughter, a smile from a stranger, and those moments when things are actually going right. I appreciate Your kindness and the fact that You made me Your child. Thank You!

Joy in Giving

*Each of you should give what you have decided
in your heart to give, not reluctantly or under
compulsion, for God loves a cheerful giver.*

2 CORINTHIANS 9:7 NIV

Lord, I thank You for Your blessings. Whether in plenty or with little, I want to be a cheerful giver. I desire to give from a full heart that serves, not reluctantly or with complaining. I long to see Your money used in ways that will bless others—through my tithing at church, giving to mission organizations, or helping the needy. I choose to give at whatever level I can—and ask You to bless it.

No Room for the Evil One

*When angry, do not sin; do not ever let your wrath
(your exasperation, your fury or indignation) last until
the sun goes down. Leave no [such] room or foothold
for the devil [give no opportunity to him].*

EPHESIANS 4:26–27 AMPC

When I can't forgive, when I can't control my anger, I know I am giving the devil a foothold into my relationships and situations. And that is not a good thing. Help me to be a forgiving person, looking for healing and reconciliation instead of bitterness and retribution. You are my life and my light. Forgive me for my attitude last night, and give me Your love and power today.

Quiet Waters

He makes me lie down in green pastures,
he leads me beside quiet waters.

PSALM 23:2 NIV

My Shepherd, my Lord, my Savior, lead me beside the still waters. Lie with me in the green pastures. Restore my soul. Lead my down the paths of *Your* choosing today. With You by my side, I fear no evil. You are my Comfort and my Guide. I am happy in Your presence. Your goodness and Your mercy are with me this minute, this hour, and this day. Thank You, Lord, for leading me here and making me whole—for being the Shepherd of my life.

Turning Obstacles into Opportunities

Lord, You know I can get upset when things don't go my way. I think a situation should play out a certain way, and when it doesn't, I lose focus and let it ruin my whole day. Help me to see obstacles as opportunities to maintain my composure. I want to learn to rise above circumstances. Remind me that in the light of eternity, a few moments of inconvenience are not worth the effort and energy I waste in negative emotional responses. Give me wisdom to see life from Your perspective—sometimes my way isn't the best way.

Servants of the Church

*Now you are the body of Christ, and members individually.
And God has appointed these in the church: first apostles,
second prophets, third teachers, after that miracles, then gifts
of healings, helps, administrations, varieties of tongues.*

1 Corinthians 12:27–28 nkjv

It's amazing how many talents people have. Please, Lord, bless those who are gifted and who are helping to serve Your body. Give them wisdom, energy, and time to do what You have designed. Help them not to get burned out. And for those who are just sitting in the pew, please speak to their hearts, urging them to set their hands to a task for You. Thank You for the gifts You have given to me. Help me to use them for Your glory.

My Past Offenses

*Keep up your reputation, God; forgive my
bad life; it's been a very bad life.*

Psalm 25:11 msg

When I look at my past, at the things I have done, I feel so unworthy of Your forgiveness, Lord. I can't even forgive myself. Please take pity upon me. Forgive me for all my past deeds. Give me a clean slate, beginning with this morning. Plant Your Word in my heart. Help me to forgive myself, as this guilt is eating away at my heart. You forgive our sins as far as the east is from the west. Thank You, God, for Your mercy! Take my sins, forgive them, and make me whiter than snow in Your eyes.

Help for a Materialistic Attitude

Keep your lives free from the love of money and be content with what you have, because God has said, "Never will I leave you; never will I forsake you."

HEBREWS 13:5 NIV

Lord, at times I'm so affected by this world—I am tempted to want what others have or long for things that I see on television. Change my attitude, Lord. Help me to understand that acquiring more "stuff" won't necessarily make me happy. Being filled with *You* brings true contentment. Teach me the joy and lasting satisfaction that come from looking solely to You, Lord.

An Attitude of Humility

Lord, without You I am nothing. I need Your mercy and grace to become all You created me to be. Help me to be content to be myself. Remind me that I am as good as anyone else, but not better than anyone else. You love equally—You love us all very much!

According to God's Will

Lord, I want to please You and do Your will all the days of my life. Forgive me when my own desires rise to the surface. I stand on the promises I read in the Bible. Set my feet firmly on Your truth. I am rooted, grounded, and determined to live by faith and do what You want me to do.

Living Water

Early the next morning. . .she went on her way and wandered in the desert. . . . Then God opened her eyes and she saw a well of water.

GENESIS 21:14, 19 NIV

Lord, thank You for being with me as I spend my quiet time in Your presence. When I am in the wilderness, You tell me not to fear. You tell me to rise in Your strength. And then You open my eyes and direct me to the living water. Lord, there is no one like You, no one who loves me as You do. I thirst for Your presence and am rewarded with Your peace. Be thou my eternal fount of blessing.

Holding That Tongue

Smart people know how to hold their tongue;
their grandeur is to forgive and forget.

PROVERBS 19:11 MSG

Whenever I bring up past deeds, I start the cycle of pain all over again. Why do I do that, Lord? Please stop me! Help me to hold my tongue, to think before I speak. Change my thoughts to those of Christ. Help me to think of the good things, the good times, I have shared with my offenders. And if there weren't any good times, remind me that You love them just as much as You love me. Help me to put their need for forgiveness above my pride. Give me Your power to live this life and be the person You want me to be.

Edify the Church

Since you are zealous for spiritual gifts, let it be for the edification of the church that you seek to excel.

1 CORINTHIANS 14:12 NKJV

Lord, I'm eager to serve You, but I'm not really sure what my gift is. And I don't want to make a fool of myself by trying something and having it be a flop. Give me guidance as to where, when, and how You want me to serve. Give me a gift that will build up Your church. Speak to me clearly as I go throughout this day and the days to come. And if there ever does come a time when You want me to bow out of a ministry, give me the wisdom to do so.

A Desire for Goodness

God, You are good, and I want to be good. You are like a rock; everything You do is perfect. You are always fair. You are my faithful God who does no wrong, who is right and fair. Let Your goodness drive my life. Help me to recognize sin and call it what it is—*sin.* No more excuses. I refuse to justify wrongdoing just because it's what I want. If it's wrong, it's not from You and I don't want it in my life. Give me a burning desire to hold on tightly to Your righteousness. In all I do, I want to please You.

God Will Provide

Therefore I tell you, do not worry about your life, what you will eat or drink; or about your body, what you will wear. Is not life more than food, and the body more than clothes? Look at the birds of the air; they do not sow or reap or store away in barns, and yet your heavenly Father feeds them. Are you not much more valuable than they? Can any one of you by worrying add a single hour to your life?

MATTHEW 6:25–27 NIV

Lord, I thank You for providing for my needs. I give You my worries and fears—those nagging thoughts about lacking money for clothes, food, and the basics of life. You feed the sparrows in the field, Lord—You'll certainly help me and my family. Your resources are limitless—You have an abundance of blessings. I praise You for Your goodness, Lord, and the faithfulness of Your provision.

Quick Forgiveness

So, chosen by God for this new life of love, dress in the wardrobe God picked out for you: compassion, kindness, humility, quiet strength, discipline. Be even-tempered, content with second place, quick to forgive an offense. Forgive as quickly and completely as the Master forgave you. And regardless of what else you put on, wear love. It's your basic, all-purpose garment. Never be without it.

COLOSSIANS 3:12–14 MSG

You have chosen me to be Your child. Help me to live that life dressed in Your love. I need Your kindness, humility, quiet strength, discipline, and definitely Your even temper. Help me to forgive others quickly and not let bitterness rot my soul. I want to forgive others as quickly as You forgive us. Thank You for the gift of forgiveness. Adorn me with Your love today and every day!

Rejoice!

*This is the day which the Lord hath made;
we will rejoice and be glad in it.*

PSALM 118:24 KJV

This is the day that You have made, Lord! I will rejoice and be glad in it! Lord, I feel Your light shining upon me. I feel Your presence all around me. I glory in Your touch! No matter what comes against me today, I know that You will be with me, so there is no reason to be afraid. All I have to do is reach for You and You are here with me. You are so good to me. Thank You, Lord, for Your goodness and Your love.

An Attitude of Repentance

The weight of my sin puts pressure on my soul. It grips me and makes me feel that I deserve punishment—and I do! But You are always forgiving. Give me the courage to tell You the truth about all I've done. Help me to always run *to* You—not away from You—when I fail. Then assure me of Your forgiveness and help me to forgive myself. Thank You for loving me, no matter what!

Water the Word

As I study the Bible, the seeds of Your Word are planted in my heart. I pray that Your truths deepen in me. Just as a tree grows strong planted by a river filled with good nutrients, I grow stronger each day through the water of Your Word.

Foundation of Truth

The church of the living God is the strong foundation of truth.
1 TIMOTHY 3:15 CEV

There is no stronger foundation than that of Your truth, which is what our church is built upon. We are not a church made up of stone, stucco, brick, or wood but of people from all walks of life. We are a church of the living God. Oh, what a glorious thing! Make our church strong, Lord, so that we can shine Your light into our community, state, and world!

Two in One

A man will leave his father and mother and be
united to his wife, and the two will become one flesh.
So they are no longer two, but one flesh. Therefore what
God has joined together, let no one separate.

MATTHEW 19:5–6 NIV

Lord, my spouse and I are two who have been united into one. I praise You and thank You for leading me to my other half. He is more than I could ever have hoped for or dreamed. Bless our marriage, bless our union, bless our lives. Help us to grow closer together with each passing year. Lead us to do what You have called us to do, as one standing before You this day.

Thank You for My Friendships

One who has unreliable friends soon comes to ruin,
but there is a friend who sticks closer than a brother.

PROVERBS 18:24 NIV

Lord, I thank You for my wonderful friends! As I think about the treasure chest of my close friends, casual friends, and acquaintances, I am grateful for the blessings and the joys each one brings to my life. Thank You for my "heart friends," my loyal sister friends who listen, care, and encourage me. They are my faithful companions. I acknowledge that You, Lord, are the giver of all good gifts, and I thank You for Your provision in friendships.

Life for Your Soul

Your Word fills my heart with joy. Lord, help me to realize my mistakes, and please forgive my hidden sins. May the words of my mouth and the meditation of my heart be pleasing in Your sight. You steady me in troubled times with the truth of Your Word (Psalm 19:7–11).

Answers in the Bible

Lord, when I feel lost and far from You, help me to find comfort in Your Word. Let Your words speak to me as though You were whispering encouragement and direction into my ear. Hold me up with the power of Your Word when I feel defeated. Give me strength when I feel drained by the pressures of my circumstances. Direct my eyes to the scriptures You want me to read for the answers I need today.

God of Peace

For God is not a God of disorder but of peace.

1 CORINTHIANS 14:33 NIV

God, sometimes life is so messy. Nothing has been going right. All I want to do is throw up my hands in frustration. But that is not of You, Lord. You are not a God of disorder but a God of peace. Help me, Lord, to be at peace now as I come to You in prayer. Help me to rest in Your presence and gain Your strength to meet the challenges of this day.

Getting Stronger Every Day

For if what is passing away was glorious,
what remains is much more glorious.

2 CORINTHIANS 3:11 NKJV

Lord, my spouse and I have been through such trials, yet each time we make it over a hurdle together, our love grows stronger. What we had in the beginning of our marriage was good, but what we have now is better. Continue to help us through the trials of this life. Help us to keep a united front before our children. And in all things, may we praise Your name for the wonders and joy of marital love.

Sunday Morning Prayer

*With one mind and one mouth glorify the God
and Father of our Lord Jesus Christ.*

ROMANS 15:6 NKJV

Unite the minds and mouths of my church, Lord, and lift them up to Your glory and the glory of Your Son, Jesus. We want to feel the power of unity as we come before You in all our ministries and worship. There is nothing like united believers coming together to seek You, all of one accord. Like the disciples at Pentecost, we want to feel the power of Your mighty wind as we gather together in Your house of prayer. Unite us, Lord, to Your glory, forever and ever!

Guided by Truth

I trust You, Lord, with all my heart. In everything I do, I acknowledge You and give Your Word first place in my life. I walk in the light of Your Word, stepping where You shine the light of truth, trusting I am in the right place at the right time to live my life according to Your purposes. I refuse to veer to the right or the left, but take comfort knowing that You are always guiding me. I listen as Your voice speaks to me, showing me the way to go.

Friends Help Each Other

If either of them falls down, one can help the other up.
But pity anyone who falls and has no one to help them up.

ECCLESIASTES 4:10 NIV

Lord, sometimes it's easier to give than to receive. I want to be a giver, to take the time to care and help my friends when they need it. And help me to learn to receive too—so that I'm not too proud to receive generosity from a friend. Give and take, Lord. . .we really do need each other.

Double Standards

Let love be without hypocrisy.

ROMANS 12:9 NKJV

Dear God, I can't believe it. I was so upset with my spouse because I thought he was taking me for granted. But it seems as if I have been doing the exact same thing. Lord, when everything was so new to our marriage, we spent so much more time together and did special things for each other, but in the passing of years, we seem to have fallen into a rut. Help us to treasure each other more, Lord, beginning this morning. Show me how I can let my spouse know he is more precious to me than silver or gold.

Strength for the Day

O Lord, be gracious to us; we have waited for You. Be their strength every morning, our salvation also in the time of distress.

ISAIAH 33:2 NASB

Oh God, I long for Your presence and Your touch. Deliver me from worry, fear, and distress. Bind me with Your love and forgiveness as I rest in You. Fill me with Your power and Your strength to meet the challenges of this day. Thank You, Lord, for the way You are working in my life. Keep me close to You throughout this day.

Joyful in Hope

Lord, I thank You for giving me hope. I don't know where I would be without You. I don't know what the future holds, but You give me the ability to be joyful even while I wait—even when I don't understand. Please help me to have a positive attitude and live with a mind-set of patience and courage as You work Your will in my life. Help me to remain faithful in prayer, Lord, and fully committed to You.

Guided by the Holy Spirit

*Let the Holy Spirit lead you in each step. . . . If the Holy
Spirit is living in us, let us be led by Him in all things.*

GALATIANS 5:16, 25 NLV

I understand, Lord, that the Holy Spirit is just waiting to lead me. Open my mind and heart and ears to His voice today. Still the constant chatter in my head that keeps reminding me of all the tasks I need to get done today. Give me the plan You have already laid out for my life. Shape me into the person You want me to be so that I can do what You have created me to do. Lead me step by step, Lord. I commit my way and my plans to Your purpose.

Finding a Secure Path

Lord, fill me with Your strength and direct my ways so I can successfully press through the temptation of sin. I want to remain obedient to Your leadership. I don't want to take Your mercy and grace for granted. Help me to focus on what is pure and holy in Your sight.

Being a Better Listener

Come and hear, all you who fear God;
let me tell you what he has done for me.

PSALM 66:16 NIV

Lord, I praise You today for all You have done for me. You have brought help, hope, healing, and restoration, and I want to tell people! Help me proclaim Your goodness, sharing the amazing ways You have come through for me. But as I speak, help me to be a good listener too. Through Your spirit, Lord, may I show I care about my friends. Give me wisdom to know when my ears should be open and my mouth shut.

Wounded and Bleeding

This one thing I do, forgetting those things which are behind,
and reaching forth unto those things which are before.

PHILIPPIANS 3:13 KJV

Lord, help my husband and me to put our past troubles behind us and look forward to the days ahead. Help us to forget some of the things that we have done and said to each other. Our marriage is wounded and bleeding, Lord. We need Your balm of love to heal it. Give us Your special touch so that we may never part. For what You have brought together shall not be put asunder. Give us strength, hope, wisdom, and guidance.

Resting in His Arms

*[Jesus] said to them, "Come away by yourselves
to a secluded place and rest a little while."*

MARK 6:31 NASB

Lord, it seems that these days I can't get enough rest. I seem to be always on the run. Calm my heart and my soul. Bathe my thoughts in Your light. I come seeking Your peace, resting in Your arms. Within this early morning silence, speak to me. Tell me what You would have me do this day. And when I come to You as night falls, lead me back to Your Word and then give me the rest I need.

Purity in My Speech

Father, You created me to be pure like You. Please forgive me when I allow the impure language of the world to come out of my mouth. I have polluted my heart by allowing those thoughts to penetrate my mind. Remove that trash from my heart as I fill up on scriptures. I am responsible for the words I speak. Help me to ask others who heard me speak like that to forgive me as well. A trash-talker is not who I want to be. When I say words like that, I am not a reflection of You.

Spirit-Filled

*I have filled him with the Spirit of God in wisdom,
understanding, much learning, and all kinds of special work.*

EXODUS 31:3 NLV

You have filled me with Your Spirit. I have been given wisdom, understanding, education, and talent for many lines of work. Show me how I can use my knowledge, understanding, and abilities to do the work You have set out for me. Show me the paths You want me to take. What do You want me to do with my hands, my life, my gifts? They are all from You, the one I want to serve.

Choosing Words Carefully

*Do you see a man who is quick with his words?
There is more hope for a fool than for him.*

PROVERBS 29:20 NLV

I did it again, Lord. I spoke before I thought, and now I have wounded my husband. According to Your Word, there is more hope for a fool than for me. I feel so terrible about what I said. I know I cannot take away the words I have spoken. All I can say is that I'm sorry. Forgive me, Father, for the words I spoke. My heart is so heavy within me. Give me the courage to ask my husband for forgiveness. And may this rift in our union be speedily mended. Heal our marriage, Lord. Give me hope.

Restoring a Broken Friendship

Above all, love each other deeply,
because love covers over a multitude of sins.

1 PETER 4:8 NIV

Lord, I thank You for Your healing balm that covers the hurt and pain I've experienced in this friendship. Your grace covers me; Your love repairs my brokenness; and You give me the ability to love again. Help me to put aside the wounds of my heart and to be a friend again. I thank You and praise You that Your love is healing and restoring. Thank You, Lord, for putting this friendship back together again.

Home, School, and Streets

Lord, there are so many dark forces within our schools, on the streets, and even in our homes. I pray for Your light to eliminate the evil among us. I know that no matter what, You will prevail, dear Jesus. You have overcome this world. You have the power to do the impossible. Show me how I can make this world a better place. Give me the heart to intercede for others and the courage to step in when and where I am needed.

Filled with Manna

*May the God of hope fill you with all joy and peace
as you trust in him, so that you may overflow with
hope by the power of the Holy Spirit.*

ROMANS 15:13 NIV

Jesus, oh, Jesus, I come to You as an empty vessel, waiting and wanting to be filled with Your joy and peace. As I trust in You to see me through this day, I am filled with hope. I expect good things to happen today as You empower me. For no matter what happens, I have Your love, forgiveness, and bounty with me always.

Record of Wrongs

*[Love] does not demand its own way. It is not irritable,
and it keeps no record of being wronged.*

1 CORINTHIANS 13:5 NLT

I can't seem to help myself, Lord. I have this list in my mind of all the things my spouse has done to hurt me. I cannot seem to let them go, and it is harming our marriage. Help me to give up on this record of wrongs. Give us a clean slate today and every day. Help me to stop bringing up the past but to just have hope for tomorrow. May the power of love erase all these wrongs and give us back the magic of yesterday.

God Gives the Power

Be careful not to say in your heart, "My power and strong hand have made me rich." But remember the Lord your God. For it is He Who is giving you power to become rich.

DEUTERONOMY 8:17–18 NLV

You are the one who has brought me to where I am today. Thank You, God, for giving me power and strength. All the blessings I have in this life come from Your hand. Continue to lead me in Your way. My ears desperately seek to hear Your voice. My heart longs for Your presence. Although I may not be rich in a worldly sense, I am rich in my love of You. Further my knowledge and increase my talents so that I can do the work You desire.

Body of Christ

Although I am less than the least of all the Lord's people, this grace was given me: to preach to the Gentiles the boundless riches of Christ, and to make plain to everyone the administration of this mystery, which for ages past was kept hidden in God, who created all things. His intent was that now, through the church, the manifold wisdom of God should be made known to the rulers and authorities in the heavenly realms, according to his eternal purpose that he accomplished in Christ Jesus our Lord (Ephesians 3:8–11 NIV).

Waiting on the Future

Know also that wisdom is like honey for you: if you find it,
there is a future hope for you, and your hope will not be cut off.

PROVERBS 24:14 NIV

Just as You promised David that he would be king, You have made promises to me for my life. I know everything You promised will happen, and I'm excited about the future. It's hard to wait on the future I know You have planned for me. Help me to find patience to be content doing what I should be doing now while on my way to achieving the purpose You have for my life.

Undying Love

Love never gives up, never loses faith, is always hopeful,
and endures through every circumstance.

1 CORINTHIANS 13:7 NLT

My love for my spouse will never die, Lord, because we believe in You. We know You have brought us together and will keep us together. We will never give up on this marriage, nor lose faith in each other, nor lose hope in our circumstances. We are in this until the end and, although we may not love every minute of it, we do love each other and You. And because of that, we are growing stronger every day. Thank You, Jesus, for the power of love!

Unwavering Faith

*Yet [Abraham] did not waver through unbelief regarding
the promise of God, but was strengthened in his faith
and gave glory to God, being fully persuaded that
God had power to do what he had promised.*

ROMANS 4:20–21 NIV

Lord, let me be like Abraham, with unwavering faith and belief in Your promises. May I be strengthened by Your Word as I meditate on it before You today, knowing and believing that You have the power to do what You have promised. I believe that You will be with me forever, that You will never leave me nor forsake me, that You will keep my head above the water, and that You love me now and to the end of my days. Thank You, Lord, for saving my soul and strengthening my faith.

Jesus' Word Power

*[Jesus said,] "The Spirit alone gives eternal life.
Human effort accomplishes nothing. And the very
words I have spoken to you are spirit and life."*

JOHN 6:63 NLT

I try and try, but my efforts accomplish nothing when I have not come first to You in prayer. I need to do things in Your strength for otherwise I am useless. I need Your power behind me when I speak. I need Your strength. Allow Your Word to speak to me. Guide my way by Your gentle voice. May my spirit and Yours become one this day.

Working to His Honor

Do everything to honor God.
1 CORINTHIANS 10:31 NLV

Everything I do and everything I have is for Your honor and Your glory—not mine! I am the ambassador of Your one and only Son, Jesus Christ. Give me that attitude today so that everyone who looks at me, hears me, and speaks to me will see His face and feel His presence. I want to become less so that He can become more. I am Your servant, Lord. Help me to serve productively and creatively. All, Lord, to Your honor!

Love for the Church

Lord, I appreciate Your love for the church. We are the works of Your hands, and our best attributes are a mirror of Your qualities. When we come together, help us reinforce those characteristics that best reveal Your nature. You are our ultimate model, but seeing others reflect Your love strengthens us as well. I pray I will reflect the light of Your love.

Your Gift Accepted

Jesus, please be the Lord and Savior of my life. I confess my sins to You. Take my life and purge me from all that is ungodly and of this world. Fill me with new life. Make me a new creature, filled with Your Spirit. Without You I am nothing, but in You I can reach my full potential.

Giving God Control of My Future

People may make plans in their minds,
but the Lord decides what they will do.

PROVERBS 16:9 NCV

Jesus, You knew that God's will was for You to give Your life so that others may experience God. You gave God total control and submitted to His will. Help me to do the same. I was created for a specific purpose. You have a plan for my life, and I want to complete everything You created me to accomplish. Help me to live my life according to Your ultimate plan.

Honoring Others with My Mouth

Don't try to impress others. Be humble, thinking
of others as better than yourselves.

PHILIPPIANS 2:3 NLT

I don't need fancy words to impress others. I only need words guided by the mind of Christ. Help me, Lord, to honor others with my speech. I want to lift people up, not bring them down. I want to bring joy to the hearts of others, not sorrow. Give me a better attitude, positive words, and encouraging remarks. Guard my mouth and, when necessary, put Your hand upon it to keep it shut.

Access to Peace and Grace

Therefore, having been justified by faith, we have peace with God through our Lord Jesus Christ, through whom also we have access by faith into this grace in which we stand, and rejoice in hope of the glory of God.

ROMANS 5:1–2 NKJV

It is my faith in You, Jesus, that keeps me sane and gives me peace. I am eternally grateful for that peace, and I thank You. My faith in You justifies me and gives me the grace I need to forgive others. Help me to do that today. Help me to look at those who have wounded me as You look at me—without blame and with love. Keep me in Your hand, and give me Your strength as I go through this day.

Respect for Others

Lord, help me radiate a warm acceptance of fellow Christians. May they delight in meeting with me. Never should they feel that I'm examining their words or actions for hidden motives. Let my attitude show respect for their opinions and their service to You. May others leave my presence feeling that they have become more solid in their walk with You. I would be pleased if they become better people because they have known me.

The Comparison Trap

Everyone should look at himself and see how he does his
own work. Then he can be happy in what he has done.
He should not compare himself with his neighbor.

GALATIANS 6:4 NLV

Lord, I keep comparing myself and my work to others, and I know that's not what You want me to do. Help me to keep my eyes on You and Your direction for my life, not on what I have or don't have. I want to be happy in this life and in what I have accomplished. Don't let me fall into the comparison trap. Thank You for the job I have now, for the pay I receive, and for the ability to serve others the best way I know how.

Need to Discipline

Discipline your children, and they will give you peace
of mind and will make your heart glad.

PROVERBS 29:17 NLT

Disciplining is easier said than done. It's true—it seems to hurt me more than it does my child. Is that how it is when You discipline me? That's something to think about. I'm sorry, Lord, for all the grief I have caused You. That makes it easier for me to pardon the grief my child causes me. Give me the right words I need to discipline my child today. Give me peace of mind so that both my heart and (eventually) his are glad!

God's Plan of Blessing

I am the Lord your God, who teaches you to profit,
who leads you in the way you should go.

Isaiah 48:17 NASB

The Bible tells me that whatever I put my hand to will prosper. I am blessed in the city and in the field, when I come into my house and when I go out of it. Your blessing on my life provides for my every need. I ask for Your wisdom, Lord. Teach me to make the right choices and decisions for my life. You make me a blessing because I belong to You.

Image of Christ

Lord, help me cultivate a strong bond with other church members. Guide me in developing confidence in them. Help me be reliable so that they too have confidence in me. It's vital that we act with one spirit and one purpose. Should we become cold toward one another, assist me in being the first to recognize the peril and to work to restore fellowship before unity is lost. Keep me focused not on myself but on You so that Christian love prevails.

Strengthened in the Faith

Just as you received Christ Jesus as Lord, continue to live your lives in him, rooted and built up in him, strengthened in the faith as you were taught, and overflowing with thankfulness.

COLOSSIANS 2:6–7 NIV

Jesus, my Jesus, thank You for always being with me, holding me up above the waters of this life, especially when the current is more than I can bear. As You uphold me, day by day, morning by morning, my faith grows. There is no one like You, Jesus. No one like You. I am strengthened during this time with You. I overflow with thankfulness and praise. What would I ever do without You in my life?

Kind Versus Cutting Words

Kind words heal and help; cutting words wound and maim.

PROVERBS 15:4 MSG

Words have cut me to the quick. Now I know how others feel when I harm them with my words. It really hurts. I feel very wounded. My stomach is filled with anger, sorrow, embarrassment, bitterness, and rage. Lord, give me a kind thought from Your Word today, scripture that will heal and build me back up. Take this sorrow from me and replace it with a spirit of forgiveness. Lift me up to Your rock of refuge.

Joyful Servant

You have done well. You are a good and faithful servant.
You have been faithful over a few things. I will put many
things in your care. Come and share my joy.

MATTHEW 25:23 NLV

I want to be a good and faithful servant sharing Your joy, but I feel like the world is bringing me down. That and my job. Help me to be faithful in what You have given me, and then, if it is Your will, put more things in my care. I want to feel and share the joy that working for and with You brings. Help me to renew my mind this morning, because my head is definitely in the wrong place. Touch me with Your compassion and grace. Fill me with Your Spirit, Your joy, Your love.

Honor for Leaders

Dear Father, a person is honored to be a Christian and doubly honored to be a Christian leader. Blessed is the church that has loyal leaders who honestly seek after the truth. They need my support. They are due my respect. Give me the humility to accept and embrace their leadership.

Knowing God Is There

God, I know You are there. Even though I can't see You with my eyes, I sense Your presence when I pray. When I feel alone, I remember Your promise to never leave me. Thank You for always making Yourself known to me when I need You.

Looking Forward

When the Spirit of truth comes, he will guide you into all truth. He will not speak on his own but will tell you what he has heard. He will tell you about the future.

JOHN 16:13 NLT

Sometimes I look back at the things that didn't turn out quite right for me. I know I shouldn't focus on wrongs done to me or opportunities missed. You have set a great life before me, and I want to embrace it without the shadow of the past. Help me see the future with joy and expectation. My hope is in *You!*

Living My Faith

If you claim to be religious but don't control your tongue, you are fooling yourself, and your religion is worthless.

JAMES 1:26 NLT

Lord, I want to live my faith before my children and others. To do that I need to be able to control my words, but sometimes, although I know this is impossible, my tongue seems to have a "mind" of its own. Help me rein in my mouth. Give me words that will lead my children to You. Help me to live a life that is rich in Your love, and may that love affect my speech. Begin with me this morning, and show me how to live this faith.

No Doubt about It

*"Have faith in God. For assuredly, I say to you, whoever. . .
does not doubt in his heart, but believes that those things
he says will be done, he will have whatever he says."*

MARK 11:22–23 NKJV

Holy Spirit, it all comes down to faith in God. Fill my heart with
assurance, with confidence, and with the promise from Jesus that
everything is possible for him who believes. Clear my mind, soul, and
spirit of any lingering doubts, even those that I have hidden. Allow
me to rest in the confidence and belief in my Savior.

Senseless Criticism

Lord, the church must do Your work, yet every action is an opportunity
for criticism. Turn me away from expressing disapproval that serves
no purpose. Teach me to appreciate what others do. Develop in me
the resolve to replace words that lead to disharmony with dialogue
that supports unity.

Thanks for My Friends

Thank You, Lord, for my friends. I appreciate that they accept me
for who I am and encourage me to grow in my relationship with You.
They are there for me when I need them, concerned for my life just
as I am for theirs. You have joined our hearts together with Your love.

Great Expectations

David. . .served his own generation by the will of God.
ACTS 13:36 KJV

Lord, I want to be like David, serving my own generation by Your will. No matter how small the job or role, fill me with great expectations that You are going to do a powerful work through me. I ask this not for my glory but to demonstrate to others the power of living in You. Imbue me with hope and thanksgiving. I do not know the entire plan You have for my life. Help me not to look too far ahead and thus miss the joy of day-to-day living. Thank You for hearing this prayer.

Three Steps to Good Speech

*Everyone should be quick to listen, slow to
speak and slow to become angry.*
JAMES 1:19 NIV

Help me with all these steps, Lord. Step number one: I need to work on my listening skills. Too often I find myself thinking of a response instead of listening to what my child is saying, and then I am rushing in with a comment or advice before he's even stopped talking. Help me to sit, listen, and wait. Step number two: Remind me to pray before I speak. I need to be patient, not letting my mouth run ahead of You. And step number three: Take away my anger. That is not of You. Calm my spirit. Give me a cool head, Your thoughts, and wise words.

The Power of Recognizing Seasons

*To everything there is a season, a time for
every purpose under heaven.*

ECCLESIASTES 3:1 NKJV

Father, I know there is a season for everything. I was born at the right season, and this is my time to live a great life. The Bible tells me there is a time for every purpose under heaven—a time to weep, a time to laugh, a time to mourn, and a time to dance. Help me to recognize the season I am in and to flow with it. I don't want to be resistant. Show me how to bend with Your leading.

The Church's Prayer for Boldness

*When they heard this, they raised their voices together in prayer
to God. "Sovereign Lord," they said, "you made the heavens and
the earth and the sea, and everything in them. You spoke by
the Holy Spirit through the mouth of your servant, our father
"'David: Why do the nations rage and the peoples plot in vain?
The kings of the earth rise up and the rulers band together against
the Lord and against his anointed one'" (Acts 4:24–26 NIV).*

Rewards of Belief

*But without faith it is impossible to please him: for he
that cometh to God must believe that he is, and that
he is a rewarder of them that diligently seek him.*

Hebrews 11:6 KJV

From the beginning of time, Lord, You have been the one. You are the Ancient of Days. I humbly come before You, earnestly seeking Your face. I am awed by Your presence and staggered by Your might and power. Hear my prayer, O Lord. Reward me with Your peace and Your strength. I believe in You.

Keep My Tongue from Evil

*For let him who wants to enjoy life and see good days
[good—whether apparent or not] keep his tongue free
from evil and his lips from guile (treachery, deceit).*

1 Peter 3:10 AMPC

I want to enjoy life! I want to see good days! But to do that, I need to keep my tongue from evil and my lips—my eternally flapping lips—from negative words, lies, and malice. There is no way I can do this by myself. No, I need Your Spirit to fill me with love and peace and joy. I need Your hand to guide me. I need Your mind to dwell within me. Give me the strength, grace, and peace I need to speak to others today in Your wisdom and Your truth.

His Work Plan

We will follow the plan of the work He has given us to do.
2 CORINTHIANS 10:13 NLV

My goal is to live the life You have planned for me. Keep me on the road to Your will. Show me the ways You want me to go. Help me avoid the worldly traps of money, discontentment, grief, envy, workaholism, and tedium. Keep me close to Your side and consistently in Your presence, ever open to hearing Your voice. Give me the power to live Your plan for me. Thank You for all You are doing in my life!

Freedom to Worship

Heavenly Father, elsewhere in the world today, Christians face danger merely because they believe in You. To assemble as a church requires courage. I'm so blessed to gather with other Christians in freedom. Meeting with others to worship rekindles my spirit. Father, I desire to take the freedom of worshipping You beyond the church meeting place. Help me extend my faith and infuse my everyday life with service to You.

Planning Ahead

The ants are not a strong people, but they
prepare their food in the summer.

PROVERBS 30:25 NASB

You know my life gets so busy that I seem to get stuck in the moment. Remind me to lift up my head and look to the future. Help me to have realistic and attainable goals. Show me how to balance my life for today while at the same time planning for tomorrow. Remind me to set my eyes on You so I can see where we're going together, with my future on the horizon.

Facing the Unknown

And now, compelled by the Spirit, I am going to Jerusalem,
not knowing what will happen to me there.

ACTS 20:22 NIV

O Lord, I feel called to take on this new challenge. I can feel the Spirit drawing me into this latest endeavor. But I don't know what's going to happen. Oh, how I sometimes wish I could see into the future. Lord, help me to have confidence, trust, and faith in Your will for my life. Help me to just put one foot in front of the other, to do the next thing, to continue walking in Your way. And when I get there, I will give You all the glory!

Hopeful Surety

Now faith is the substance of things hoped for, the evidence of things not seen.

HEBREWS 11:1 KJV

Although I cannot see or touch You, Lord, You are here with me. You are waiting to hear my prayer, ready to do what's best for me. You know me better than I know myself. Thank You for spending these precious moments here with me as I open my heart and share my hopes, dreams, fears, and needs with You. Increase my faith as I hope in You.

Choosing the Best Course

Lord, effective Christian action grows in an atmosphere of encouragement. In our work, many questions arise, such as which programs to support and how best to direct our efforts. I pray Your grace will be with all those in my church. Steer us along the best course between the rocks of hard-line fanaticism and the murky waters of caution. May we work as an agreeable team to bring honor to Your name.

Forgiving My Friend

*"Be alert. If you see your friend going wrong, correct him.
If he responds, forgive him. Even if it's personal against you
and repeated seven times through the day, and seven times
he says, 'I'm sorry, I won't do it again,' forgive him."*

LUKE 17:3–4 MSG

I've about had it, Lord. I keep getting hurt by my friend. I don't know how much more of this I can take! Is this friendship even worth all this pain? Lord, please calm me. Give me the right attitude. Your Word says that no matter how many times I am offended, if my friend apologizes and says she'll never do it again, I am to forgive her. Well, You're going to have to give me this power, because I have none of my own left. Please work, live, and love through me. Help me to forgive my friend.

Devoted to God's Word

Today I choose Your Word, Lord. Your way is just and right. I will take the path You have chosen for me, and I will walk in the direction Your Word tells me to go. Help me to follow You with all my heart. Help me to keep my heart right so I always do what pleases You. Help me to keep Your commandments. Show me biblical truths. I am devoted to Your Word. I take it to heart so I will not sin against You.

A Habit of Selflessness

Since Christ suffered while he was in his body, strengthen
yourselves with the same way of thinking Christ had.
The person who has suffered in the body is finished with sin.

1 PETER 4:1 NCV

Lord, I've been self-centered. There are times when I felt like the world revolved around me. Forgive me for such selfishness. I won't die if everything doesn't go my way. Help me not to react so emotionally when something doesn't turn out as I expected. Give me compassion for others and a sense of selflessness to serve them.

For My Pastor

God, thank You for giving me a spiritual leader who loves me and You. Help them to always speak Your truth and never stray from it. Surround them with wise counsel, and give them a heart that listens to counsel that ultimately comes from You. Keep them close to You, filled with Your compassion for the people You have placed in our church. Protect them from criticism. Help them to be watchful over our church family, discerning what is Your best. Bless them and their family in everything they do.

Faith and Wellness

Rise and go; your faith has made you well.

LUKE 17:19 NIV

Nine simple words—*"Rise and go; your faith has made you well."* What a treasure they are! Keep them in my mind and heart today. Help me to retain their sounds, meaning, and import. May I rise from this place of prayer full of faith that heals my mind, body, spirit, and soul. Thank You, Lord.

Support of Fellow Believers

When [Paul] would not be dissuaded, we gave up and said, "The Lord's will be done."

ACTS 21:14 NIV

Sometimes those who don't know You think that believers like me are crazy. But we're not. We just know that when You call us to do something, when You put a challenge before us, we are to go forward with no fear. We are bold in You, Lord! How awesome is that! And thankfully, fellow believers encourage us, knowing that if it is Your will, all will be well. What would I do without that support? Thank You for planting my feet in a nice broad place, surrounded by fellow believers who love and pray for me.

Easily Offended

I will give you a new heart and put a new spirit within you.
I will take away your heart of stone and give you a heart of flesh.

EZEKIEL 36:26 NLV

Lord, I have such anger within me for all the wrongs done me all day long. Even when I'm out in traffic and someone cuts me off, I'm really miffed. Or when my family comes to the dinner table and no one appreciates how hard I've worked to make this meal but complains about every little thing, I just want to scream! Give me that new heart. Empty this heart of stone, the one so easily offended. Fill it with Your love.

To Be a Support to Others

Lord, help me to encourage others every day. Help me to share what I have with others and encourage them. You are my strength, so I will lean on You as others lean on me. Help me to build their faith instead of tearing it down. Help me to be positive and uplifting when people share their troubles with me. When people leave my presence, I want them to feel better than when they came to see me.

For Good Health

Say to him: "Long life to you! Good health to you and your household! And good health to all that is yours!"

1 SAMUEL 25:6 NIV

Lord, I thank You for my good health. It is a blessing. I pray for Your power to sustain me as I take care of myself by eating healthy food, drinking enough water, and making movement and exercise a part of my daily life. Give me the self-control and motivation I need to make wise choices to support the health of my mind, my spirit, and my body. Please keep me from injury and illness. Keep me safe, I pray.

Our Help

Our help is in the name of the LORD, who made heaven and earth.

PSALM 124:8 NKJV

I need look no further than You, Lord, to help me. It is Your name that I trust. It is Your power that will help me meet this challenge. After all, You made heaven and earth. You made me. You know the plan for my life. You have equipped me to do what You have called me to do. Help me not to rely on myself but on You and Your power. That is what is going to give me victory in this life. Thank You for hearing and answering my prayer.

Walking in God's Wisdom

*Listen, my son, accept what I say, and the years of your life
will be many. I instruct you in the way of wisdom and lead
you along straight paths. When you walk, your steps will not
be hampered; when you run, you will not stumble. Hold on to
instruction, do not let it go; guard it well, for it is your life.*

PROVERBS 4:10–13 NIV

Lord, I want to do what You have created me to do. I come to You
today, seeking Your direction for my life. I have my own ideas of how
You want me to serve You, to enlarge Your kingdom here on earth,
to provide for myself, my family, and my church. But I need Your
wisdom. Which route should I take? When shall I begin? How shall I
go? Lead me, Lord, into the waters You have chartered for my life.

To Hear His Voice

God, I want to hear Your voice. I want to know You are speaking to
my heart about Your will for my life. Just as the sheep follow the
shepherd's voice and pay no attention to the stranger's words, help
me to shut out strange voices so I may hear You clearly. Give me
patience to listen and not talk. What You have to tell me is much more
important than what I have to say. Help me to practice Your presence and wait on You. Nothing is more important than time with You.

No Guilt Trips, Please

Now is the time to forgive this man and help him back on his feet. If all you do is pour on the guilt, you could very well drown him in it. My counsel now is to pour on the love.

2 CORINTHIANS 2:7–8 MSG

I don't know why, Lord, but I just keep bringing up old offenses and throwing them into the faces of those who have hurt me. I know that's not how You want me to behave. If I keep on this course, there's no telling how many people I will alienate from my life. And I'm not being a very good example of a Christian. Help me to forgive others and not remind them of past deeds. Help me to pour out Your love to all.

My Armor

I will not trust in my bow, nor shall my sword save me. But You have saved us from our enemies, and have put to shame those who hated us. In God we boast all day long, and praise Your name forever.

PSALM 44:6–8 NKJV

I do not trust in my talents, diligence, money, education, luck, or others to help me meet this challenge. I trust in You. My power is in the faith-based boldness that only comes from knowing You intimately. With that weapon in my arsenal, there is only victory ahead. Those who say I cannot do what You have called me to do will be put to shame. But that's not why I continue to meet this challenge. I go forward because I want to bring glory to you. It is in You that I boast all day long. I praise Your name, my Strength and my Deliverer.

Wholeness and Right Living

Do not be wise in your own eyes; fear the Lord and shun evil.
This will bring health to your body and nourishment to your bones.

PROVERBS 3:7–8 NIV

Lord, help me to be a person who takes care of herself. As I look to Your wisdom for right living, may I enjoy a healthy body. I need to take responsibility for my actions—what I choose to put in my mouth and my mind is up to me. Help me to make wise decisions and to be a good steward of myself, the "temple" you have given me. Help me not to abuse my body but to care for it as You would want me to.

Seeking the Right Knowledge

God, You know everything. All I want to know is already known by You. Teach me to seek truth in a way that pleases You. I don't want to use what I *think* I know of You or Your Word to look good in front of other people. Help me to keep my motives pure. I never want to seek knowledge that is separate from You. Help me to know You by listening to You and observing what You do. I don't just want to know Your Word; I want to put it into practice. I want to live it out loud every day.

Wisdom of Creation

By wisdom the LORD laid the earth's foundations, by understanding he set the heavens in place; by his knowledge the watery depths were divided, and the clouds let drop the dew.

PROVERBS 3:19–20 NIV

God, Your creation is so awesome. Everywhere I look, I see Your handiwork. You have made it all. You have made me. Continue to mold me and shape me into the person You want me to be. Give me knowledge and wisdom in how best to serve You.

Make Me Bold

On the day I called, You answered me; You made me bold with strength in my soul.

PSALM 138:3 NASB

Sometimes I feel like a ninety-five-pound weakling when it comes to my faith. I let my doubts and fears overtake me and then find myself shrinking from the challenges You put before me. Lord, I ask You to make me bold. Give me the strength to take on all comers and to do what You want me to do. Dispel the darkness that surrounds me. Warm me with the light of Your face. Bring me to where You want me to be. Give me strength in my soul!

Needing Mercy

People who conceal their sins will not prosper, but if they
confess and turn from them, they will receive mercy.

PROVERBS 28:13 NLT

Lord, I am so mad at myself. I have been doing wrong and hiding it from everyone. I even imagined I could hide it from You, but You know all. Lord, please forgive me for not admitting my sins to You. Help me to do better. I don't want to live this way. Sometimes I can't stand myself. Please help me to turn from this behavior. Give me Your never-ending mercy and eternal lovingkindness.

Discovering Leadership

Heavenly Father, I want to understand how to become a leader. Jesus led by serving others. He freely gave of Himself to show us the way to truth. Teach me what it takes to lead as I begin by following You and the leaders You placed in my life. Give me a heart to serve and the patience to not take shortcuts in the lessons You want me to learn.

Getting Rid of Stress

Cast all your anxiety on him because he cares for you.

1 PETER 5:7 NIV

Lord, help me to find relief from stress in my life. I need to value rest and make time to relax—and I need Your power to do so. I cast my cares on You, my Burden Bearer. Help me to deal with the toxic, unhealthy relationships in my life. Give me the strength to say no when I need better emotional boundaries. And please help me find joy again in the things I like to do—unwinding with music, taking a walk, calling a friend, or learning a new hobby. Calm me, and renew me, Lord.

God Looks at the Heart

But the LORD said to Samuel, "Do not consider his appearance or his height, for I have rejected him. The LORD does not look at the things people look at. People look at the outward appearance, but the LORD looks at the heart."

1 SAMUEL 16:7 NIV

Some people look at me and say, "There's no way you can do this." But with You I can do anything, Lord. You don't just look at my appearance. When You look at me, You look directly at my heart. I know that You have made me to use my particular talents to accomplish particular tasks here on earth. You know my purpose, my path. Help me use all my resources to meet this challenge before me. All to Your glory!

Faith in the Invisible

*By faith we understand that the worlds were
prepared by the word of God, so that what is seen
was not made out of things which are visible.*

HEBREWS 11:3 NASB

I cannot see my future, Lord. I must trust in Your wisdom to guide me through these uncharted waters. Although I cannot see what the future holds, You see it, Lord. You have it all planned out. Open my ears to Your voice and my eyes to Your creative vision for my life. Help me to see where You want me to go. Then give me the courage to steer my life in that direction.

Learning in the Circumstances

God, teach me how to tune out the voice of my circumstances, the busyness of my life, and the noise surrounding me. My situation hasn't changed, but my attitude has. My hope is in You. Help me to focus on Your promises instead of the circumstances that are shouting at me. I open my heart to listen to Your instruction. Teach me to go to the still waters of Your Spirit and find strength. Peace like a river speaks to me.

Forgive Me!

If I say, "My foot slips," Your mercy, O Lord, will hold me up. In the multitude of my anxieties within me, Your comforts delight my soul.

PSALM 94:18–19 NKJV

God, I've messed up again. I can hardly forgive myself. But when my foot slips, Your mercy holds me up! Forgive my offenses, Lord. Take away this feeling of anxiety within me. Help me to stop belittling and berating myself. My confidence is so low. Comfort my soul with Your presence, Your love, Your Spirit. And as You keep forgiving me, help me to forgive others.

In God's Strength

I have strength for all things in Christ Who empowers me [I am ready for anything and equal to anything through Him Who infuses inner strength into me; I am self-sufficient in Christ's sufficiency].

PHILIPPIANS 4:13 AMPC

It's amazing—I can do all things through You! You give me the power! You give me the energy! You give me the ways and the means! As I lie here in Your presence, I feel all the energy emanating from You. Oh, what a feeling! Give me that strength I need to accomplish the goals You set before me. Plant the words "I can do all things through God—He strengthens me!" in my heart forever and ever.

Time and Motivation for Fitness

*Do you not know that your bodies are temples of the
Holy Spirit, who is in you, whom you have received
from God? You are not your own; you were bought at
a price. Therefore honor God with your bodies.*

1 CORINTHIANS 6:19–20 NIV

Lord, I need more time—and motivation—to get in shape. I want to
have a fitness routine, but my schedule is crazy; there is always so
much to do every day. Show me how to make movement a priority
in my life so I will feel better, look better, and have more energy. I
want to honor You with my body in my physical health. Lord, I want
to be a woman of balance not extremes. Help me to care for my
body and be a wise steward of this resource You've given me all the
days of my life.

Developing a Passion for the Bible

Father, help me to make daily Bible study as much a part of my life
as eating. Remind me that the Bible is more than a book, that it
contains words revealing Your love for me. Holy Spirit, speak to my
heart and tell me what I need to discover each day. Bring what I've
read back to my memory so I can meditate on what Your Word is
saying to me personally.

The Breath of Life

The Lord God formed man of the dust of the ground, and breathed
into his nostrils the breath of life; and man became a living soul.

GENESIS 2:7 KJV

It is through You that I have life. Each and every day, You breathe life into my soul. You send my spirit soaring into unknown heights. Thank You for the gift of life. I dedicate it to Your service. Where would You like me to go? What shall I do? Which path shall I take? Speak to me as I remain still, listening for Your voice, awaiting Your direction.

A Solid Foundation

Therefore everyone who hears these words of mine and puts them
into practice is like a wise man who built his house on the rock.

MATTHEW 7:24 NIV

Lord, I come before You to ask that You would establish our home on the solid rock of Your love. Please be our cornerstone. I pray that our family would be rooted in love, grounded in grace, and rich in respect for one another. Help us to be a family that reaches up to You, reaches in to support one another, and reaches out to the world around us. May we stand firm as a family built on a foundation of true faith.

Eating Right

Go, eat your food with gladness, and drink your wine with a
joyful heart, for God has already approved what you do.

ECCLESIASTES 9:7 NIV

Lord, I thank You for filling the earth with a bounty of food. I praise You for the variety of fruits, vegetables, proteins, and carbohydrates you provide for sustaining life. Help me to make a priority of eating a nutritious blend of foods, to drink enough water, and to avoid overindulging in junk. I pray for the time to shop and cook balanced meals. Please help me find food that is healthy and good-tasting and the will to eat in moderation.

Being Passionate about the Right Things

Forgive me, Lord, when I am tempted to love things that are pretty to look at or make me feel good about myself. I want to stay focused on You. Help me to eliminate anything that competes with knowing You. Remind me when my natural desires are not in line with what You would have me pursue. I want to love what You love and hate what You hate. Help me to get rid of things in my life that keep me from serving You with all that I am.

For a More Positive Attitude

*For the Lord searches all hearts and understands
all the intent of the thoughts.*

1 CHRONICLES 28:9 NKJV

Lord, You look into my heart and see the truth of how I think and feel. I won't pretend anymore, because I know I can be real with You. Help me to let go of the things that have hurt and angered me. I don't want those things to be my focus. I want to be focused on You and what You have planned for my life today. Help me to do what I need to do without grumbling, complaining, or pointing fingers at others. Fill me with Your joy and strengthen me with Your love.

Serve the Lord

*But if serving the Lord seems undesirable to you,
then choose for yourselves this day whom you will serve. . . .
But as for me and my household, we will serve the Lord.*

JOSHUA 24:15 NIV

Lord, this world offers so many choices of things or people to whom we could give our allegiance. We will choose not to bow to the gods of materialism or selfishness. Instead, please give us the strength to serve You. As we humbly bow before You, we ask that You would provide for all our needs so we can be a means to help and supply the needs of others through our service and hospitality.

The Right Focus

We do not know what to do, but our eyes are upon You.

2 CHRONICLES 20:12 AMPC

Help me, Lord, to focus on You in all I say and do, in every decision I make, and in every direction I take. Help me to make the most of each opportunity. My life's aim is to serve, obey, and seek You. I do not know what to do, but my eyes, Lord, are upon Your heavenly face, and in this I rejoice!

The Fullness of the Holy Spirit

Thank You, Lord, for Your Holy Spirit. I trust that the Holy Spirit leads and guides me in every area of my life. You sent the Holy Spirit to comfort me and teach me all things. He directs my steps and helps me to make wise life choices. He shows me God's best for my life. I set my heart on the promise of His presence and diligently listen to His leading.

Living with Pain

Great is the Lord and most worthy of praise;
his greatness no one can fathom.

PSALM 145:3 NIV

Lord, I choose to praise You through this pain. You are great, and there is no one worthy of Your honor and glory. "Heal me, LORD, and I will be healed; save me and I will be saved, for you are the one I praise" (Jeremiah 17:14 NIV). I give you this discomfort, and I ask in the name and power of Jesus that You would take it away. Help me and heal me completely from my hurt. Let my heart ache only for the comfort and healing balm of Your presence.

A Place of Love and Respect

Show proper respect to everyone, love the family
of believers, fear God, honor the emperor.

1 PETER 2:17 NIV

Lord, may our home be a place where we show love and respect to one another. Help us to value each member of our family and everyone we welcome into our home. We may not always agree; we may have different opinions. But I pray that we would extend kindness to others and seek to view them as significant, worthy, and valuable. We choose to honor others in our home because we honor You.

Transforming My Thoughts

*May the words of my mouth and the meditation of my heart
be pleasing to you, O Lord, my rock and my redeemer.*

PSALM 19:14 NLT

Father, Your Word says I can choose what to think about. Help me to refuse thoughts that keep me prisoner to things in my past or to worries about my future. My hope is in You. You are my strength and my shield. Transform my thoughts with the truth of Your Word. When I read the Bible, help me to remember Your Word. Then when my mind wanders to matters that bring me down, I will recall what You have to say about them.

Seeing the Unseen

Lord, I am learning so much. I want to see You in the small moments in my life today. I don't want to take anything for granted, so show me the majestic beauty of Your creation. I want to experience You in all I see. Help me to see the unseen. Give me wisdom to read and understand Your Word. Give me discernment so I know the right things I should do. Open the eyes of my spirit so I can see clearly from Your perspective.

You Made Me!

Thy hands have made me and fashioned me.
PSALM 119:73 KJV

You have known me since the beginning. You know my doubts and fears, yet You love me still. Sometimes I feel as if I am adrift in confusion. I need You to lovingly urge me on past that darkness and into Your light. Thank You for Your patience. Help me to create a life with You; help me to be not just a lump of clay sitting on a shelf, out of harm's way but unused. Continue to shape me and mold me into the person You want me to be.

Hospitality

Share with the Lord's people who are in need. Practice hospitality.
ROMANS 12:13 NIV

Lord, I thank You for my home. Show my heart opportunities to open this home to others. I want to share what You've provided for me. As I practice hospitality, may Your love shine through my life. However my home compares with others', I thank You for what I have. I am grateful that Your spirit is present here. Give me a generous, open heart, and use my home for Your good purposes.

When Healing Does Not Come

*I consider that our present sufferings are not worth comparing
with the glory that will be revealed in us. . . . And we know
that in all things God works for the good of those who love
him, who have been called according to his purpose.*

ROMANS 8:18, 28 NIV

Lord, I have prayed, and healing hasn't come. It's hard to know why
You do not heal when You clearly have the power to do so. Please
help me not to focus on my present suffering but to be transformed
in my attitude. May I revel in the glory that will be revealed in me
through this and, ultimately, when I am with You in heaven. I do not
understand, but I choose to praise You anyway. Give me the peace,
comfort, and assurance that all things—even this—will work for my
good and for Your glory.

Increase My Faith

Jesus, You promised that if I believe when I pray according to our
Father's will, I can have what I ask. It's so hard to believe sometimes, especially when it seems my prayer is taking a long time to
be answered. Forgive me for not trusting You. You have never failed
me, and sometimes I forget that. Help me to stand in faith, knowing that I will see the results of my faith. Remind me that answers
come in Your time, not mine. You are the finisher of my faith, so I
hold tight to You.

Guarding My Mind

*You will keep in perfect peace those whose minds
are steadfast, because they trust in you.*

ISAIAH 26:3 NIV

Thank You for the helmet of salvation to protect my mind. As I spend time with You and in Your Word, I know I will become more like You. I will guard my mind and refuse to allow negative thoughts to have power over me. Your Word is my weapon to fight the thoughts that oppose who I am in Christ. I will be careful about the things I see and hear, because I know they can open my mind to positive or negative thinking. Help me to focus on truth.

Living in Harmony

*They broke bread in their homes and ate
together with glad and sincere hearts.*

ACTS 2:46 NIV

Lord, may our home be a place of harmony. Let gladness and sincerity be hallmarks here as we share meals together, entertain, live, laugh, and play together as a family. I pray against discord and fighting, and I pray for peace. Give each of us an agreeable spirit. When the challenges of life come, help us to love and support one another with empathy, kindness, and love.

Set Apart and Appointed

Before I formed you in the womb I knew you,
before you were born I set you apart; I appointed you.

JEREMIAH 1:5 NIV

Oh God, before I was even conceived, You knew me and loved me. You have set me apart for a special purpose, for a way to achieve Your ends. I am nothing without You, yet You ask me to be a part of the grand plan. Even knowing my weaknesses, You have loved me. Give me the vision You have for my life so that I may best know how to serve You. Here I am, Lord. Use me!

Praying God's Words

I don't have to worry about my problems today. You are giving me the answers I need to change my life. Hebrews 4:12 (NIV) says, "The word of God is alive and active. Sharper than any double-edged sword." When I speak and pray the scriptures, I am agreeing with You in what You want to do on the earth and in my life. I attach my faith to Your words, and You give life to the desires of my heart. As I pray today, I know Your power is released to answer my prayers.

Perseverance in Prayer

As you know, we count as blessed those who have persevered.
You have heard of Job's perseverance and have seen what the Lord
finally brought about. The Lord is full of compassion and mercy.

JAMES 5:11 NIV

I feel like I've been praying forever for a situation that does not seem to be changing, Lord. I feel like Job: Here I am on my knees in prayer while the entire world dissolves around me. But I know that You are in control. You know all things. So once again, I lift my concern up to You, confident that You will handle the situation in Your timing.

A Place to Grow Up

To equip his people for works of service, so that the body of
Christ may be built up until we all reach unity in the faith and in
the knowledge of the Son of God and become mature, attaining
to the whole measure of the fullness of Christ. Then we will
no longer be infants, tossed back and forth by the waves, and
blown here and there by every wind of teaching and by the
cunning and craftiness of people in their deceitful scheming.

EPHESIANS 4:12–14 NIV

Lord, I ask that our home would be a place where we can mature in every area of life. Just as we grow up physically, help us to grow up emotionally and spiritually too. We don't want to be childlike and immature, tossed back and forth by the waves of life's storms or the deceitful ideas of people who seek to mislead us. Strengthen us in the knowledge of Your ways, and help us to experience Your love and wisdom.

An Attitude of Mercy

*For the weapons of our warfare are not carnal but mighty in
God for pulling down strongholds, casting down arguments and
every high thing that exalts itself against the knowledge of God,
bringing every thought into captivity to the obedience of Christ.*

2 CORINTHIANS 10:4–5 NKJV

Lord, when others treat me unfairly, judge me, or take something I
feel I deserved, I want to get even. I want to fight for what is mine, but
then I feel You urging me to show mercy. It's hard for me to do that.

Unsaved Loved Ones

It's been difficult serving You when my family members don't know
You. I can't seem to make them understand. I don't want to argue or
defend my relationship with You anymore. Help me to choose words
and actions that let them see You in me. I pray they see the difference
You have made in my life and that they'll come to know You too.

Never Say Can't

The LORD said to me, "Do not say, 'I am too young.'
You must go to everyone I send you to and say whatever
I command you. Do not be afraid of them, for I am
with you and will rescue you," declares the LORD.

JEREMIAH 1:7–8 NIV

I know what You want me to do, Lord. I hear Your voice telling me how You want me to serve. Help me to put aside my doubts, misgivings, and fears. I want to go where You command. I know You will be by my side through it all.

A Safe Place

My people will live in peaceful dwelling places,
in secure homes, in undisturbed places of rest.

ISAIAH 32:18 NIV

Lord, I ask that You would be our strong defense and protect our home. May this be a place of safety, comfort, and peace. Guard us from outside forces, and protect us from harmful attacks from within. I pray that the Holy Spirit would put a hedge of protection around our home and family. Lord, we look to You as our refuge, our strength, and our security.

The Healing Edge

*People. . .begged him to let the sick just touch the edge
of his cloak, and all who touched it were healed.*

MATTHEW 14:35–36 NIV

Lord, when I connect with You, when my body is filled with Your power and love, nothing can harm me. I am healed from within. Fill me now with Your presence. Heal my body, soul, and spirit. I praise Your name for You are the one that heals me, saves me, loves me! Thank You for giving me life!

For Peace in My Family

You have promised the peace that passes understanding. Thank You that Your Spirit lives in and with us. My family is blessed in all we do. I thank You, Lord, that Your peace goes with us. No matter how much chaos is going on around us, we can rest and rely on You. Help us not to get caught up in the moments when it seems the world is spinning out of control. Remind us to fix our minds and hearts on You and live in Your strength today.

God's Word Is Truth

To the Jews who had believed him, Jesus said, "If you hold to my teaching, you are really my disciples. Then you will know the truth, and the truth will set you free."

JOHN 8:31–32 NIV

Thank You, Lord, that Your Word is true. Sometimes it's hard to discern truth from a lie or even from the half-truths that bombard me daily from the television, radio, magazines, and popular culture. I want to know the truth and live it. Help me to look to Your steady and solid Word, not to this world, for my life instruction manual. I thank You that You will never lead me astray, that You never lie to me, and that You always keep Your promises.

Encouraging Words

Gracious words are a honeycomb, sweet to the soul and healing to the bones.

PROVERBS 16:24 NIV

Lord, I pray that we would speak encouraging and kind words in our home. Help us to build one another up—never to tear one another down. Help us not to be so self-absorbed that we forget to ask how others around us are doing. Like honey, may the words from our mouths be sweet to the soul and healing to the bones. Help us to be positive, peaceable, and considerate. Thank You for giving us words that restore.

For with God, I Can!

With your help I can advance against a troop;
with my God I can scale a wall.

PSALM 18:29 NIV

With You, my awesome God, all things are possible. I can do anything through You. I can climb that mountain, take that job, or whatever You are calling me to do! Like Joshua, I can be strong and courageous. No one can stand against me because You are by my side.

Facing a Family Crisis

It is so hard dealing with this family crisis. Lord, teach me how to face these issues in a positive way. I feel so alone. Thank You for being with me. I can't be the one to fix this problem for them even though I'd like to. You're the only one who can. Bring people across my path who I can talk to about this, people who can support me and lift me up. Help me to focus on what I have to do, and keep me from becoming distracted. I give it all to You right now. I know You won't let any of us down.

Strength in Weakness

*Therefore I take pleasure in infirmities, in reproaches,
in needs, in persecutions, in distresses, for Christ's
sake. For when I am weak, then I am strong.*

2 CORINTHIANS 12:10 NKJV

It's a paradox, but it is Your truth. When I am weak, I am strong because Your strength is made perfect in my weakness. Because You are in my life, I can rest in You. With Your loving arms around me, I am buoyed in spirit, soul, and body. When I am with You, there is peace and comfort.

A Family That Prays Together

*He and all his family were devout and God-fearing; he gave
generously to those in need and prayed to God regularly.*

ACTS 10:2 NIV

Lord, I want our family to pray together more often. We need to put You first because You are the source of life—and You are worthy of our firstfruits of time and attention. Help us make spending time with You a priority. I pray that meeting with You together will draw us closer to You and to one another. I believe You have so much more for us. I ask for Your blessing as we seek to honor You in this way.

Light for Understanding

Your word is a lamp for my feet, a light on my path.

PSALM 119:105 NIV

Lord, Your Word is a lamp in my darkness—a flashlight on the path of life that helps me see the way. Your words enlighten me with wisdom, insight, and hope, even when I cannot see where I am going or how things will turn out. I'm so glad that You know the right direction. You have gone before me and are always with me, so I don't need to be afraid. I choose to follow Your leading.

Kind Versus Cutting Words

Words have cut me to the quick. Now I know how others feel when I harm them with my words. It really hurts. I feel very wounded. My stomach is filled with anger, sorrow, embarrassment, bitterness, and rage. Lord, give me a kind thought from Your Word today, scripture that will heal and build me up. Take this sorrow from me, and replace it with a spirit of forgiveness. Lift me to Your rock of refuge.

No Fear

This is what the Lord says—he who made you, who formed you in the womb, and who will help you: Do not be afraid.

ISAIAH 44:2 NIV

You've made me the way I am for a reason, for a purpose. You are the author and the finisher of my faith. For now and always, You are there to help me. I am not afraid when my hand is in Yours. Thank You for leading me out of the darkness and into the light of Your Word.

Wise Stewardship

The Lord is my strength and my shield;
my heart trusts in him, and he helps me. My heart
leaps for joy, and with my song I praise him.

PSALM 28:7 NIV

Lord, I thank You for the household You have entrusted to my care. Help me to be a wise steward of my resources, of all that You have provided. Help us to take care of our things, to keep them clean and in good repair. May we use our money wisely, may we share freely of Your blessings, and may we spend our time toward positive ends that bring glory to Your Name.

His Promise of Restoration and Health

*For I will restore health to you, and I will
heal your wounds, says the Lord.*

JEREMIAH 30:17 AMPC

You are the healer of our wounds, the one who restores spirit, soul, and body. Thank You for blessing my life. As I spend this time with You, I feel Your touch upon me. You are my gentle Shepherd, always trying to keep me from harm. Thank You, Jesus, for coming into my life, for making me complete, for restoring me to God. All praise and glory to my *Jehova-Rapha*, the Lord who heals!

For Stability in Relationships

Lord, I ask for You to stabilize my family relationships. Help us to overcome the things that cause us to push one another away. Teach us to be steady and strong for one another. Show us how we can honor one another. Soften our hearts, and help us to forgive if we feel we've been wronged.

God's Word Is Powerful

For the word of God is alive and active. Sharper than any double-edged sword, it penetrates even to dividing soul and spirit, joints and marrow; it judges the thoughts and attitudes of the heart.

HEBREWS 4:12 NIV

Thank You for Your life-changing words that reveal the true condition of my heart. I can't hide it from You for You already know everything. But with Your conviction come repentance and forgiveness. You accept me as I am and give me the grace and power to make real and lasting changes in my life. The Word of God is living and active. That's why it has so much power. I give You my thoughts and attitudes and ask for healing.

Managing Your Household

She watches over the affairs of her household and does not eat the bread of idleness.

PROVERBS 31:27 NIV

Lord, I thank You for the wisdom you give me each day to watch over the affairs of my household. Give me energy to accomplish my work and to keep our home organized and running smoothly. Help me to be a good time manager and to stay centered on Your purposes. I need to get my tasks done, but I also want to nurture and cherish my relationships. Empower me, Lord. Help our home to be a place of order, peace, and enjoyment.

Opportunity Knocks

And who knows but that you have come to the kingdom
for such a time as this and for this very occasion?
ESTHER 4:14 AMPC

Like Esther, I have been brought to this place in my life for such a time as this. I expectantly wait to hear from You, to see You, to serve You. Thank You for this opportunity to make a difference in this world and to show others how awesome You are. Direct me on the path of Your choosing. My feet are waiting to follow Your command.

When My Family Frustrates Me

God, I love my family members, but they frustrate me. I want to be there for them, and I want them to be there for me. But they make choices I don't understand. Instead of confronting them in anger, teach me how to pray for them and speak to them with Your love. Like me, they are still growing in their relationship with You and in their knowledge of Your Word. When conflicts arise, show me how to find solutions that benefit all of us according to Your purpose and Your plan for our family.

Relentless Praying

[Daniel] continued kneeling on his knees three times a day, praying and giving thanks before his God, as he had been doing previously.

DANIEL 6:10 NASB

"As he had been doing previously"—what amazing words! Help me to be like Daniel, Lord. When faced with arrest and execution, when all seemed bleak and hopeless, he didn't panic but did as he had always done. He came before You on his knees, giving thanks. Keep me close to You, Lord. Enter my heart as I kneel at Your throne.

Blessing for a New House

The Lord's curse is on the house of the wicked, but he blesses the home of the righteous.

PROVERBS 3:33 NIV

Lord, please bless this new house. We dedicate it to you in the name of Jesus. We ask that You would bring protection and safety to this place. Fill each room with Your loving presence, Your peace, and Your power. May we treat one another with respect, with warmth and welcome for others. Use this house to bring glory to Your name, Lord. May all who come here feel at home.

Wisdom in Interpretation

*Do your best to present yourself to God as one
approved, a worker who does not need to be ashamed
and who correctly handles the word of truth.*

2 Timothy 2:15 niv

Lord, I am Your student. Teach me to read Your Word, meditate on it, and apply it to my life. Give me a hunger for spending time with You and wisdom when I teach Your Word to others. I want to be a person who correctly handles the Word of Truth. I ask the Holy Spirit to enlighten me and give me understanding that I may live right and bring glory to Your name.

Trusting God for Stability

God, I've done everything I can to make things right, and now I am doing what I should have done first—I'm letting go! Do what You will with everything I've held so tightly to. I don't need to be in control. I give it all to You now. Help me to leave it with You and not pick it back up. I'll do only what You ask me to do—nothing more.

My Desires

Delight thyself also in the Lord: and he shall
give thee the desires of thine heart.

PSALM 37:4 KJV

Lord, as I come before You today, delighting in Your presence, I ask for Your divine guidance. You know the desires of my heart—to know, love, and live in You. Show me the way You want me to go. Give me the courage to face the future, knowing that You go before me. I need never be afraid.

I Am God's Child

The Spirit of God, who raised Jesus from the dead, lives in you.

ROMANS 8:11 NLT

Jesus, thank You for providing the way for me to belong to Your family. Everyone who accepts You and believes in You becomes a child of God. I am born of God—not from natural birth but by spiritual birth. You are my example, and I will do my best to follow in Your footsteps. I want to be like You and our heavenly Father. I want to have the same character and nature. I receive Your gift of inclusion in the greatest family of all eternity.

Healer of Hearts, Binder of Wounds

He heals the brokenhearted and binds up their wounds.

PSALM 147:3 NASB

My heart is broken. I no longer have any strength. Fill me with Your power. Put Your arms around me. Let me linger in Your presence, bask in Your love. You are all I need. For without You, I can do nothing. Quench my thirst with Your living water. Feed me with Your bread of life. Nourish me deep within. I come to You in despair. I leave filled with joy.

Breaking Fear's Grip

God, I admit that sometimes fear grips me. I want to be strong in faith, but sometimes circumstances are just too much. Help me to recognize fear and draw strength from You so I can break fear's grip when it begins to overwhelm me. Forgive me when I try to handle life on my own. I want to depend on You, but sometimes it's hard to let go. Teach me how to trust You, since I know You are more than able to deal with any circumstance I encounter.

To Know God's Will

For this reason, since the day we heard about you,
we have not stopped praying for you. We continually ask
God to fill you with the knowledge of his will through all
the wisdom and understanding that the Spirit gives.

COLOSSIANS 1:9 NIV

Lord, I want to know Your will for my life. Enlighten me with wisdom, discernment, and understanding. I need to know when to stay and when to go, when to speak and when to close my mouth. Fill me with the knowledge of Your best for me—right now and in the future. As I seek to follow you, help me to obediently and joyfully accept Your answers.

A Matter of Significance

To them God willed to make known what are the
riches of the glory of this mystery among the Gentiles:
which is Christ in you, the hope of glory.

COLOSSIANS 1:27 NKJV

Jesus, help me to find my identity in You. I know that my relationship with You is significant. As I read the Bible, give me an understanding of who You created me to be. Point out the true identity that has been given to me through the gift of salvation and my relationship with You.

Serving with Purpose

David. . .served the purpose of God in his own generation.
ACTS 13:36 NASB

Dearest God, You have a purpose for my life. You have plans to prosper me. I put my life, my heart, my spirit, and my soul in Your safe hands this minute, this hour, this day. Within Your firm grasp, I need not worry about what tomorrow may bring. I know You have my life planned. I just need to keep close to You and to keep walking in Your way, looking neither to the right nor the left but straight ahead toward You.

Love of Money

Dear God, I come to You this morning with a heavy heart. I feel as if I have let my quest for financial security take my eyes off of You. Help me to put aside my fear of never having enough. Replace it with trust in You. Take away my seemingly insatiable appetite for more and more gain, and replace it with the power of contentment. Free me from the snare of greed, and lead me into greater faith in You.

You Have Heard My Prayers

This is what the Lord, the God of your father David, says:
I have heard your prayer and seen your tears; I will heal you.

2 Kings 20:5 niv

As I come to You today, I know that You hear the prayers and praises I offer. You have seen my tears. You know the calamity that has befallen me. You are my all in all. Give me the strength to endure this pain. Give me Your healing touch. Fill me with Your light and life. I thank You for working in my life, moment by moment, day by day.

Making Prayer a Priority

But blessed is the one who trusts in the
Lord, whose confidence is in him.

Jeremiah 17:7 niv

Lord, I feel like a withered plant with dry, brown leaves. Help me connect with You in prayer so I can grow strong and healthy, inside and out, like a vibrant green tree. You are my source of living water. Teach me to be still, to listen, to absorb what You want to reveal to me in this time of inward filling. In this holy conversation, may I find freedom, peace, and joy—and a closer walk with You.

Give Me Joy

The precepts of the Lord are right, giving joy to the heart.
The commands of the Lord are radiant, giving light to the eyes.

PSALM 19:8 NIV

Lord, Your words are right and true; they bring joy to my heart. I need more joy in my life. Happiness comes and goes, but joy is deep and lasting. This world can take so much out of me with the cares of the day, pressures from my job, and commitments I've made. I need Your true joy despite my circumstances and my feelings. Your commands illuminate me, so I can sing Your praises and live revitalized each day. Thank You for Your joy, Lord.

The Right Heart-Set

A heart-set is like a mind-set, Lord. Each morning I need to ask myself where my heart is. Is it set on making lots of money so that I can buy things I don't really need? Is my heart set on showing how much better off I am than my neighbor? Rather, I pray that my heart is set on You and what You want me to do each and every moment of the day. Help me to not get caught up in this "me" world. I want my life to be all about You.

A Future for Me

Consider the blameless, observe the upright;
a future awaits those who seek peace.

PSALM 37:37 NIV

Lord, I am Your child, a child of peace. When someone strikes me on the left cheek, I turn my head and give them the other. I can only do this through Your power. Nothing can harm me when I am living so close to You. Now, with the next breath I take, give me the gift of stillness, of silence, as I put my future, my hopes, my dreams into Your capable hands.

Living a Life of Love

"Love your neighbor as yourself."

MATTHEW 22:39 NIV

Lord, I want to live a life of love! Show me what true love is—Your love—so I can receive it and give it away to others. Teach me to care for my neighbor as I would care for myself. Let love be my motivation for action. Help me to speak kind, encouraging words and to bless others with my actions as well. I thank You that Your amazing, unconditional, accepting love sustains me.

Never Alone

I will never leave you nor forsake you.

JOSHUA 1:5 NIV

Your Word says that You will never leave me, but right now I feel all alone. I am afraid of what lies before me. Help me to know, beyond a shadow of a doubt, that You are with me. You are my Good Shepherd. With You by my side, I need not fear. Fill me with Your presence and Your courage as I greet this day.

Truthful Friendship

The Bible says that as iron sharpens iron, so true friends sharpen the hearts and minds of one another. God, I want to have relationships that are true and honest. Help me to tell the truth in the most gentle and positive way. I want my friends to know the truth about me and about the things that concern them. When they ask my advice, help me to share truth and wisdom from You that will help them grow in their relationship with You. Show them that I love them and want Your best for their lives.

Joy

Our mouths were filled with laughter,
our tongues with songs of joy.

PSALM 126:2 NIV

Lord, thank You for the gift of laughter! I thank You for the joy You bring into my life through a child's smile, a luscious peach, a hot bath, and a good night's sleep. Help me remember that when I am "looking up" to You, Lord, I can have a more optimistic outlook and be a more positive person. Keep my eyes on You, not myself or my circumstances, so I can live with a lighter, more joy-filled heart.

A Person of Wisdom

Blessed are those who find wisdom, those who
gain understanding, for she is more profitable than
silver and yields better returns than gold.

PROVERBS 3:13–14 NIV

Lord, I want to be a person of wisdom, not foolishness. Help me to make right choices and conduct myself in a manner worthy of Your name. I pray that I would be honest and upright in my daily life so my actions reflect who You are. Help me to act with integrity so I become a person who keeps promises and commitments.

Sweet Wisdom Breeds Hope

So shall the knowledge of wisdom be unto thy soul:
when thou hast found it, then there shall be a reward,
and thy expectation shall not be cut off.

PROVERBS 24:14 KJV

You, O Lord, give me hope for the future. Your presence fills me. I seek Your wisdom to renew my spirit and help me face the challenges of this life. I have great expectations. I believe that You are working in my life and good things await me today. May I further the plans for Your kingdom as You lead me through this life and time.

Prayer of Discernment

That same Spirit who raised Christ from the dead lives in me. Thank You that my heart is sensitive to Your purposes and plans for my life. I clearly distinguish between right and wrong; I see the light and walk in it. I trust You, Lord, with all my heart and refuse to rely on my own understanding in any matter. Help me to choose Your way, the right way, every time. I am determined to know You and discern Your voice when You're speaking to me, just as a child knows the voice of a parent.

Calling All Angels

He will order his angels to protect you wherever you go. They will hold you up with their hands so you won't even hurt your foot on a stone.

PSALM 91:11–12 NLT

Oh, what a tremendous God You are! You have commanded Your angels to surround me. Right now they are protecting me, guarding me from danger. You will not let anything that is not of Your will touch me. You won't even let me trip over a stone. With Your heavenly host surrounding me, there is no need to fear. Still my rapidly beating heart as I take one breath. . .then another. . .then another, here in Your presence. You are an awesome God. You are *my* God. Thank You for always being there—here—in my heart.

Confidence

The Lord will be at your side and will keep your foot from being snared.

PROVERBS 3:26 NIV

Lord, help me to have more confidence—not in myself but in You. I don't want to be proud or conceited, but I don't want to be a doormat, either. Give me a teachable heart. You have so much to show me, and I want to learn Your ways. Learning and growing, I am alive! I am totally dependent on You, Lord. Full of Your Spirit, I can stand confident and strong.

A Right Perspective

What agreement is there between the temple of God and idols? For we are the temple of the living God. As God has said: "I will live with them and walk among them, and I will be their God, and they will be my people."

2 CORINTHIANS 6:16 NIV

Father, sometimes I wish I looked different because there are things about my body that I don't like. Remind me that You knew what I looked like long before I was born. I am wonderfully made by Your hand. Help me to be thankful for how You designed me. I want to be a good steward of the body You gave me. Help me to nurture it, respect it, and celebrate it. My body doesn't belong to me—it belongs to You! And what I do with it reflects on You.

Addressing Bad Habits

Father, I don't want to talk to You about this habit I have, but I know I need to. Help me to see the real reason for my habit, and show me how to heal the pain that drives me to keep doing it. Give me the courage to keep trying if I mess up. Help me to stay strong and just say no to guilt.

To Be There for Others

Thank You, Lord, for the rich blessings You have given me in my understanding friends. Help me always to be there for them. No matter what they are facing, give me the patience to stand with them, no matter how long it takes. Help me to remember them in my prayers, and remind me that my relationships with them are centered in our faith in You.

In God's Arms!

*Then I said to you, "Do not be terrified; do not be afraid of them.
The L*ORD *your God, who is going before you, will fight for you, as he
did for you in Egypt, before your very eyes, and in the wilderness.
There you saw how the L*ORD *your God carried you, as a father
carries his son, all the way you went until you reached this place."*

DEUTERONOMY 1:29–31 NIV

No matter what I face today, You, Lord, are going before me. You
appear before my very eyes. You will lead me through the desert,
sustaining me with Your living water. When I am tired, You will carry
me like a child until I reach the place You have intended for me.

The Value of Rest

*Do you not know? Have you not heard? The L*ORD *is the everlasting
God, the Creator of the ends of the earth. He will not grow
tired or weary, and his understanding no one can fathom.*

ISAIAH 40:28 NIV

Lord, I come to You for respite. Like a rest in music breaks the ten-
sion, I need a break too. Whether it's a quarter rest, like a nap, or a
whole rest, like a good night's sleep or a day off, may I find healing
and strength in quietness and solitude. Give me the courage to be
still, to cease striving, and to be with You. Replenish me in Your
presence, Lord.

In God I Trust

But even when I am afraid, I keep on trusting you. I praise your promises! I trust you and am not afraid. No one can harm me.

PSALM 56:3–4 CEV

When all is said and done, it simply comes down to this, Lord: In whom do I trust? If I allow messages from the devil to fill my mind, I will be defeated. You have overcome this world; You have overcome the evil one. Plant Your Word in my mind so that there is no room for the fears that threaten to consume me. Help me to remember that I need never fear, for You are with me.

Forming a Habit of Prayer

I am so thankful that I can talk to You, Lord. Time spent with You in prayer feeds my spirit and fills me with Your power and strength. I am always tempted to come to You with my list of things I want, when I should just sit and listen to what You have to say. Help me to be more diligent with my prayer time.

For a Pure Heart

The temptations in your life are no different from what others experience. And God is faithful. He will not allow the temptation to be more than you can stand. When you are tempted, he will show you a way out so that you can endure.

1 CORINTHIANS 10:13 NLT

God, create in me a pure heart and a right spirit. Show me all my wrongdoings. Give me the strength to resist the lies that distort my thinking when I try to justify sin. Make me new, like the first day I was born into the kingdom of God. As I fill my mind with Your truth from the Bible, help me to renew my mind with right thinking. Show me Your ways, and instruct me in all I do. Guide me with Your eye, and direct me with Your truth.

Dealing with Pride

For by the grace given me I say to every one of you: Do not think of yourself more highly than you ought, but rather think of yourself with sober judgment, in accordance with the faith God has distributed to each of you.

ROMANS 12:3 NIV

Lord, Your Word says that we are not to think of ourselves more highly than we ought, but to think of ourselves with sober judgment, in accordance with the faith You have given us. Help me not to have pride, arrogance, or conceit in my heart—but when I do, please forgive me. Humble me, Lord, and lift me up to be a willing servant. With my eyes on You, not on myself, may I see the needs in the lives of others.

A Future Hope

There is surely a future hope for you,
and your hope will not be cut off.

PROVERBS 23:18 NIV

Nothing will cause me dismay; nothing will discourage me with You by my side, O Lord of my life. Help me to seek Your advice, Your Word, before I speak, before I move, before I act. Guide me through this maze of life, Lord, with the assurance that You always walk before me. Embed this truth deep within my soul.

Making Forgiveness a Habit

God, You always forgive me, but sometimes it's hard to forgive myself. I feel so ashamed when I continue to do things that I've committed to You and myself not to do. The Bible says that once I ask You for forgiveness, You don't remember my sin—but I do. It comes to mind day after day and brings guilt and shame with it. Cleanse my heart and mind of this guilt, Lord. Help me to forgive myself. Help me love myself in spite of my faults—the way You love me.

Fear of My Enemies

I will call upon the LORD, who is worthy to be praised; so shall I be saved from my enemies. . . . For by You I can run against a troop, by my God I can leap over a wall. As for God, His way is perfect; the word of the LORD is proven; He is a shield to all who trust in Him.

PSALM 18:3, 29–30 NKJV

Today, Lord, I feel as if my enemies are surrounding me and there is no way out. But that is wrong thinking, wrong feeling. That is not the truth of the situation. The truth is that, with You, nothing is impossible. With You, I can do anything—even leap over a wall. There is nothing to fear. Your way is perfect; and your Word, on which I totally rely, is filled with promises made and kept. Today I face my enemies and stand with You, surrounded by Your shield on each and every side. I take my refuge in You.

You Don't Have to Be Perfect

For the law was given through Moses; grace and truth came through Jesus Christ.

JOHN 1:17 NIV

Lord, when I struggle with perfectionism, help me to break this bondage in my life. I know it's a good thing to want things to be right, but it's possible to go too far. I want to live in Your grace, not under the "law" that keeps me under this burden. Heal me, Lord, from judging myself and my actions too harshly—and fearing the judgment of others. Help me to see, Lord, that because of Your mercy and grace, I am good enough.

To Yield to God's Standards

*I urge you, as foreigners and exiles, to abstain from
sinful desires, which wage war against your soul.*

1 PETER 2:11 NIV

Lord, You know me better than I know myself. You know my internal struggles and the things that challenge me deep within my soul. You created me, and You know what I need. I surrender what I want for what You know I need. You have the highest standards, and I want to meet them. I give myself to Your will and hope with great expectation to live my life according to the standards You have set in place.

Add to Your Faith

Father, You have given me great and precious promises. With these promises I can live separate from the world, removed from its evil desires. Because You have given me these blessings, I am determined to add to my faith goodness, knowledge, and self-control today. Help me to grow in patience and in service for You. Help me to show kindness and love to others. As I nurture these things in my life, help me to know You more.

No Fear for the Future

*Keep sound wisdom and discretion: so shall they be life unto thy
soul, and grace to thy neck. Then shalt thou walk in thy way safely,
and thy foot shall not stumble. When thou liest down, thou shalt not
be afraid: yea, thou shalt lie down, and thy sleep shall be sweet.*

PROVERBS 3:21–24 KJV

Do not allow my foot to stumble, Lord. Eliminate the obstacles of
worry and fear that line the path before me. Give me hope and
courage to face my future. Give me a clear mind to make the right
decisions. And, at the end of this day, give me the peace of sweet
slumber as I lie down within Your mighty arms.

A Thankful Heart

*Rejoice always, pray continually, give thanks in all
circumstances; for this is God's will for you in Christ Jesus.*

1 THESSALONIANS 5:16–18 NIV

Lord, You are my God—and it is my joy to give You my inner heart.
Cleanse me, fill me, heal me, and help me to live with a joyful, thankful
heart. I want to be a woman of prayer. I want to make a difference
in my world. For all You are and all You do, I am grateful. I give You
praise for the blessings in my life.

One Way Out

Trust in the Lord with all your heart and lean not on your own understanding; in all your ways submit to him, and he will make your paths straight.

PROVERBS 3:5–6 NIV

Lord, I am so afraid of what this day may bring. So many times I have tried to make this situation right, and nothing seems to be working. I cannot figure a way out anymore. Help me to trust in You—not just halfway but the whole way. I don't understand what's happening, but I acknowledge Your presence in my life and Your ability to make all things right.

A Habit of Laughter

Father, I haven't had a good belly laugh in a long time. I don't mean to take life too seriously. Bring times of refreshment into my life. Remind me to look for opportunities to experience the joy of laughter. Point them out to me, and then help me to let go and have a good time. Laughter seems to release stress and adjust my attitude. Inject me with funny thoughts when I need to relax and have a good laugh.

Standing with God

Everyone deserted me. May it not be held against them. But the Lord stood at my side and gave me strength. . . . And I was delivered.

2 TIMOTHY 4:16–17 NIV

All of a sudden, I am as alone as David when he stood before Goliath. But I am not going to be mad at others for deserting me. I don't need them. All I need is You. You are my Lord, my Savior, my Deliverer, my Rock, my Refuge. You are by my side. I can feel Your presence right here, right now. Oh, how wonderful You are! Thank You for giving me the power I need. Thank You for never leaving me.

The Joy of Knowing Jesus

But let all who take refuge in you be glad; let them ever sing for joy. Spread your protection over them, that those who love your name may rejoice in you.

PSALM 5:11 NIV

Jesus, knowing You brings me joy! I am so glad that I am saved and on my way to heaven. Thank You for the abundant life You provide. I can smile because I know that You love me. I can be positive because You have the power to heal, restore, and revive. Your presence brings me joy—just being with You is such a privilege. You are awesome, and I delight to know You and tell others about You.

Unknown Future

*Indeed, how can people avoid what they
don't know is going to happen?*

ECCLESIASTES 8:7 NLT

Dear God, I don't know what lies before me. I feel plagued by the what-ifs that tumble through my mind and pierce my confident spirit. Allow me to let You fill my soul. Help me to be confident in Your wisdom and power to guide me so that, although You have concealed from me the knowledge of future events, I may be ready for any changes that arise.

Devoted to Truth

Lord, when I am devoted to Your truth, it becomes clear which things do and don't belong in my life. I don't want to believe the lie that truth is relative. Show me truth in black and white. Help me to break the habits that keep me from living a life pleasing to You. As I am tempted to repeat an old habit, remind me that You are there with me, ready to help me let go. Help me to live according to Your truth.

Leaning on the Word

For you have been my hope, Sovereign LORD,
my confidence since my youth.

PSALM 71:5 NIV

Lord, since I've known You, You have been my hope—most times my only hope. You give me confidence to face the day. Sometimes I'm afraid to step out the door, to watch the news, to read the paper. But at those times, all I need to do is remember Your Word and trust in that. Your Word is my confidence and my strength. When those arrows of misfortune come my way, help me to lean back and rest in Your Word, committing Your promises to memory, strengthening my spirit and my soul.

Finding Joy in God's Presence

The LORD has done great things for us, and we are filled with joy.

PSALM 126:3 NIV

Lord, draw me closer to You. In Your presence is fullness of joy—and I want to be filled. Knowing I am loved by You makes me glad; I cannot imagine life without You. With You, there is light; without You, there is darkness. With You, there is pleasure; without You, there is pain. You care. You comfort. You really listen. Here, in Your presence, I am loved, I am renewed, and I am very happy.

To Go beyond the Four Walls

*For where two or three gather in my
name, there am I with them.*

MATTHEW 18:20 NIV

Jesus, I need Your help. We have become comfortable inside our church. Where is the desire to tell others about You? Teach us how to go outside the four walls of our church building. Speak to the hearts of the people within our church family. Share Your vision to reach out into the community through them. Give us the desire to demonstrate Your love to those who are hurting. Grow in us an eagerness to reach and transform lives through the love of God within us.

Life in Your Word

God, Your Word breathes life into me. Help me to be committed to Your Word, to study it, and place it in my heart. Bring Your words back to me as I go through my day. Instruct me, encourage me, and fill me with Your words.

Shattered Plans

*My days have passed, my plans are shattered. Yet the desires of my
heart turn night into day; in the face of darkness light is near.*

JOB 17:11–12 NIV

O God, all my plans are in ruins. I don't understand why all this is
happening. The things I have desired are out of my reach. I feel like
Job. Yet at the end of his days, as he kept his confidence in You, You
blessed Job, making his life even richer than before. Wipe the tears
of frustration and disappointment from my eyes, Lord. Help me to
keep my focus on You and not my troubles or my worries about what
the future will bring.

Living Daily with Delight

*You will go out in joy and be led forth in peace;
the mountains and hills will burst into song before you,
and all the trees of the field will clap their hands.*

ISAIAH 55:12 NIV

Lord, I thank You for the joy You bring every day. Whether I go out
or stay in, joy is with me because You are there. Lead me forth today
in peace. May all of creation—even the trees of the field—praise you
as I praise You. Help me to live with a lighter heart and a positive
attitude, despite the distractions and duties that seek to steal my
joy. I choose You. Help me to live daily with Your delight.

Prayer for Protection

So do not throw away your confidence; it will be richly rewarded.
. . . But we do not belong to those who shrink back and are
destroyed, but to those who have faith and are saved.

HEBREWS 10:35, 39 NIV

Lord, help me to be a frugal Christian and not throw away my confidence in You. Fill my spirit with power and courage so I can face this day with You beside me, ready to protect me at a moment's notice. I believe in You. You will save me, bringing me through the fire and flood, the storm and desert. You are holding my hand, shielding me from the evils of this world. Thank You, Lord, for walking with me through the shadows of this valley.

Accepting Responsibility for My Actions

It would be easier to deny my mistakes to myself and to others, but I want to be a person of integrity and honor. Truth is important to You—and to me. Lord, give me the courage to take responsibility for my actions. I know that with each action there are consequences, both positive and negative. Help me to think before I act and to listen to Your instruction and direction for decisions I make, no matter how big or small.

Daring to Dream

Take delight in the LORD, and he will give
you the desires of your heart.

PSALM 37:4 NIV

Dear Giver of Dreams, I believe you've placed dreams within me that are yet to be realized. Teach me to delight myself in You as I pursue the desires of my heart. Show me Your perfect will. May I move as far and as fast as you wish, never less or more. Grant me the wisdom I need to accomplish Your plans for my life and the humility to give You the glory in them.

Obedience Leads to Joy

As the Father has loved me, so have I loved you.
Now remain in my love. If you keep my commands, you will
remain in my love, just as I have kept my Father's commands
and remain in his love. I have told you this so that my joy
may be in you and that your joy may be complete.

JOHN 15:9–11 NIV

Lord, Your Word says that if we obey Your commands, we will remain in Your love. I want to serve You out of an obedient, not a rebellious, heart. Just as Jesus submits to You, Father, I choose to submit to You too. Obedience leads to a blessing. Empower me, encourage me, and give me the will to want to make right decisions—decisions that lead to a better life and greater joy.

God's Plans

But the plans of the LORD stand firm forever,
the purposes of his heart through all generations.

PSALM 33:11 NIV

You have led me to this place where I now lie before You, seeking Your presence and Your face, Your guidance and Your strength. Your plans for my life stand firm, although they are as yet unrevealed to me. With one glance, You see all the generations that have gone before, that are present now, and that will come in the future. You see it all! Allow me to rest in the knowledge that each and every day You go before me and that, in the end, all will be well with my soul.

Accepting Responsibility for My Words

My words are powerful. They can add to or take away from someone's life. I want to be a positive influence in the lives of those around me. I want to encourage them with Your goodness and love. I want to be truthful, and sometimes it's hard to say certain things, but I'm asking You to help me speak the truth in love. For those I have hurt with my words, help me to take responsibility, apologize, and set things right with them. Lord, put a guard over my mouth so I speak Your words in love.

Let It Be

*Trust in the LORD with all your heart, and lean not on
your own understanding; in all your ways acknowledge
Him, and He shall direct your paths.*

PROVERBS 3:5–6 NKJV

I acknowledge that You are in control of everything, Lord, and that the things You want me to accomplish today will get done. I want to walk in Your will and not in mine. I want to lean on Your Word and take Your paths. I can only do that by putting my total trust in You as I go through this day. I want to be like Mary. I want to be Your servant, saying, "Let it be to me according to your word" (Luke 1:38 NKJV). So, Lord, help me to accomplish what You want me to do today and let the rest be.

Deal with Anger

*"In your anger do not sin": Do not let the sun
go down while you are still angry.*

EPHESIANS 4:26 NIV

Lord, I need Your help in dealing with my anger, whether I am simply annoyed, a little mad, or downright furious. I want to handle this feeling in healthy ways. Help me to process my emotions and not let them fester inside me. Help me to control my temper and talk about what bothers me in calmer ways. Show me how to give my anger to You so I can live in peace with others.

Knowing God's Will

Do not conform to the pattern of this world, but be transformed by the renewing of your mind. Then you will be able to test and approve what God's will is—his good, pleasing and perfect will.

ROMANS 12:2 NIV

Lord, I commit my aspirations to You. Give me the courage to work toward my own goals and not be swayed by the opinions of others. Renew my mind and my spirit so I will be able to test and approve what Your will is—Your good, pleasing, and perfect will. I don't have to be afraid that I will miss it—I can know that You bring people and circumstances into my life for a reason. Thank You for the assurance that You will direct me into Your good purposes.

Choose Life

Jesus, You offered me life, not just life after death but eternal life that started the day I asked You to live in my heart. Help me to remember that every choice I make is a choice for life or for death, for blessing or cursing. I don't want to live one day less on the earth because of a poor choice I made. Help me to make every decision count.

Man's Plans, God's Purpose

*Many plans are in a man's mind, but it is the
Lord's purpose for him that will stand.*

PROVERBS 19:21 AMPC

You know the plans of my mind and the desires of my heart. But as
Your Word says, it is Your purpose that will rule the day. Help me
to step aside if I am blocking Your way. Help me to keep confident
in Your Word and in Your plan for my life. I await Your instructions
for the day.

Forgive Each Other

*Get rid of all bitterness, rage and anger, brawling
and slander, along with every form of malice.*

EPHESIANS 4:31 NIV

Lord, I don't know why forgiveness can sometimes be so hard. We
need Your help to get rid of bitterness and anger in our marriage.
Help us to build each other up instead of putting each other down,
even when it seems we deserve the latter. Teach us grace. Help us
to forgive one another and to be kind and compassionate, because
we know Christ forgave each of us.

Change My Thoughts

Don't be like the people of this world, but let God change the way you think. Then you will know how to do everything that is good and pleasing to him.

ROMANS 12:2 CEV

Lord, I don't want to be like the people of this world, running around at breakneck speed, trying to multitask until I'm so deep in the darkness I can no longer see the light of Your face. It's not all about doing; it's about being. Change *my* way of thinking to *Your* way of thinking. I take this to-do list and place it in Your capable hands. Help me to see this list through Your eyes. Show me clearly the steps I am to take today.

Facing the Truth

Lord, I know I need to change a lot of things in my life. Thank You for accepting me as I am, where I am today. You see the potential of who I can be even when I can't see it. Show me the things in my heart that You want to change. Open my eyes; I don't want to pretend anymore. Help me see the truth so You can make me new!

The God Who Cares

You discern my going out and my lying down;
you are familiar with all my ways.

PSALM 139:3 NIV

Lord, I thank You that You are the God who cares! You want the best for me, and You are constantly designing the next steps of this journey of my life. Powerful, yet gentle and kind, You delight in giving us dreams and the resources to achieve our goals. I pray for dreams that are worthy and wonderful. Empower me, gracious God, to be a woman of action who trusts You.

Fun and Friendship

Two are better than one, because they have a good return for
their labor: if either of them falls down, one can help the other
up. But pity anyone who falls and has no one to help them up.

ECCLESIASTES 4:9–10 NIV

Lord, I thank You for the bond of friendship in our marriage. I enjoy talking and sharing life with my husband. Thank You for our laughter and joy. Help us to keep our attitude positive, to smile and have fun together. Give us time to reconnect on a playful level—in sports, games, travel, or working together around the house. Keep us connected in love and friendship, and help us to truly enjoy each other.

Christ's Riches

*My God shall supply all your need according
to His riches in glory by Christ Jesus.*

PHILIPPIANS 4:19 NKJV

Oh Lord, what a promise You have made to me, that You will supply all I need through Christ. He is my Good Shepherd; with Him I shall not want! Help me to rest confidently in the assurance that in Your time my prayers will be answered. Let my prayer time be more than utterances of what I desire but a time of fellowship with You, knowing that You will provide what I need.

An Imitator of God

Father, my relationship with You affects my personality in amazing ways. Many people have a negative idea of what it means to be a Christian. Forgive me when I've failed to be like You. I want to be so full of Your presence that others see You in everything I say and do. I never want anything I do to reflect negatively on You. I want to be like Jesus, of whom people said, "Truly this was the Son of God!" (Matthew 27:54 NKJV).

My Main Desire

One thing I have desired of the LORD, that will I seek: that I may dwell in the house of the LORD all the days of my life, to behold the beauty of the LORD, and to inquire in His temple.

PSALM 27:4 NKJV

Lord, help me to keep the main thing the main thing—and that is to seek first the kingdom of God, beholding Your beauty, inquiring in Your temple. That is all that is truly important, not whether I get all my work done at home, the office, or church. As I receive requests for my time and ability, give me wisdom to say yes and no in accordance with Your will.

Genuine Authenticity

*These people show honor to me with words,
but their hearts are far from me.*

MATTHEW 15:8 NCV

Lord, help me to be a true reflection of Your heart in all that I do. Help me to take off the mask when I'm tempted to hide my true self. Remind me that my actions should not be for attention, praise, or position. I want my motives to always be pure. Help me to discern my real intentions when I decide to do something. Keep me honest, and remind me that I represent You in the choices I make. In everything I pursue, help me above all to be committed to my relationship with You.

The Giver of Guidance

*I will instruct you and teach you in the way you should
go; I will counsel you with my loving eye on you.*

PSALM 32:8 NIV

Lord, I appreciate Your wise hand of guidance. You instruct me and teach me in the way I should go; You counsel me and watch over me. What a blessing! What a privilege! No one knows my inner heart and life dreams like You, Lord. Still me. Help me to listen so I can hear Your direction. And when I hear, give me the courage to walk forward knowing You are always near. You are with me every step of the way, Lord.

Finding Courage

Jesus, thank You for the courage to live my life following Your example. I can do all things through You who gives me the power to succeed. I refuse to be intimidated by what others say, think, or do. I live my life according to our Father's will and the Holy Spirit's instruction. Help me to declare to others the freedom I have found in You so I point the way to You. Equip me to lead others to follow You.

Watching with Hope

But as for me, I watch in hope for the Lord,
I wait for God my Savior; my God will hear me.

MICAH 7:7 NIV

I watch and wait expectantly, Lord, for You to answer the petitions I make to You today. I bring them to You, mindful of the way You are always there, ready to listen, ready to advise, ready to answer. Give me the gift of patience as I wait for Your response. Help me not to run ahead of You but to wait and pray and hope.

Living Sacrifices

Therefore, I urge you, brothers and sisters, in view of God's
mercy, to offer your bodies as a living sacrifice, holy and
pleasing to God—this is your true and proper worship.

ROMANS 12:1 NIV

Here I am, Lord, lifting myself up to You this morning. I want to serve You. I live to please You for I love You with all my strength, soul, mind, heart, and body. I dedicate myself, my time, and my service to You. Show me the path You want me to take so that at the end of my days, when I see Your smiling face, You will say, "She did what she could."

Capturing Thoughts

We are taking every thought captive to the obedience of Christ.
2 CORINTHIANS 10:5 NASB

God, it seems like I need a reminder every moment of the day to listen to Your voice. I keep getting caught up in the world of busyness, and that's not where You want me to be. Help me not to be overwhelmed by the demands of this society but to be open to Your voice. I want to hear You speak to me all throughout the day. I want to do only what You want me to do each moment. Remind me to take each thought captive to Christ so that I am not misled, going somewhere or doing something that is not of You.

To Live in Christ

In Your love and mercy, You gave me life when You raised Christ from the dead. I was lost and alone, but You found me. You picked me up and gave me all the benefits of Your own Son, Jesus. Thank You for Your incredible kindness. All I had to do was believe and receive this gift. I can't take credit for it—it was all You! Father, continue to make me new each day in Christ.

Trusting God's Wisdom

*For the LORD gives wisdom; from his mouth
come knowledge and understanding.*

PROVERBS 2:6 NIV

Lord, what a blessing it is to be able to come before You—the wisest, most intelligent Being in the universe. I have direct access, straight to the top. Thank You for giving me wisdom and direction even when I can't see the way. Knowledge and understanding come directly from Your mouth, Lord, and You delight to enlighten us. I praise You and ask for continued insight as my dreams become achievable goals.

To Live What I Believe

Walk by the Spirit, and you will not carry out the desire of the flesh.

GALATIANS 5:16 NASB

Lord, forgive me when my choices don't line up with what I say I believe. Help me to nurture Your Word in my heart so I grow to maturity. Teach me Your ways, and give me understanding of Your instructions. Allow the values of my faith to affect every area of my life. Convict me of sin when I am tempted to stray from truth. Help me to stay committed to living what I believe as I grow in faith and in my relationship with You.

In His Time

*The Lord upholdeth all that fall, and raiseth up all those that
be bowed down. The eyes of all wait upon thee; and thou
givest them their meat in due season. Thou openest thine
hand, and satisfiest the desire of every living thing.*

PSALM 145:14–16 KJV

Lord, sometimes I don't understand why it takes so long for You to answer some of my prayers. At times Your answers are immediate; but on other occasions, I need to keep coming before You, asking over and over again for You to meet my need. Help me to grow during this time, Lord. Give me the confidence to ask and keep on asking.

Pure Motives

Lord, help me to examine my motives in pursuit of friendship. Sometimes I think a relationship with a certain person might help me look better in the eyes of others. I am ambitious, but I know it's wrong to use people to get what I want. You supply everything I need. Help me to maintain right and pure relationships before You.

A Fresh Start

I want a fresh start with my family. Help us to get past our faults and mistakes. Stop me when I'm tempted to bring up past stories that caused hurt, pain, or embarrassment. Remind us of the good times we all share. Help us to be caring and compassionate with one another. Give me the desire and ability to forgive the past, and help them to forgive me.

With Him Each Moment

*But more than anything else, put God's work first and do
what he wants. Then the other things will be yours as well.*

MATTHEW 6:33 CEV

I can't seem to find any time, Lord. It's always rush, rush, rush. I need to remember that I am already with You in the heavenlies. Calm my heart. Help me to breathe slower. I want to relax here at Your feet. I want to smell Your perfume, touch Your robe, hear Your voice. When I do Your work today, everything else will then fall into place. I lean back against Your knees, waiting to hear Your voice.

Sharing My Challenges

*Be an example to the believers with your words,
your actions, your love, your faith, and your pure life.*

1 TIMOTHY 4:12 NCV

Father, You know all I have gone through in my life, all of my hurts and pains. I know I went through those difficulties for a reason, perhaps to encourage others. Help me to be quick to share with anyone who might benefit from what I have endured. Help me to share how I learned to trust in You as You brought me through each challenge. Strengthen those people with boldness and courage. Give me the words to encourage them to hold tightly to You during their hardships.

Make Love Your Aim

*The goal of this command is love, which comes from a
pure heart and a good conscience and a sincere faith.*

1 TIMOTHY 1:5 NIV

Lord, in all my activity to achieve my goals, through the effort and
the trusting, may my highest aim be love. Love is Your greatest commandment. Fill me with Your unconditional and accepting love, and
empower me to care deeply and well for others. May the love I give
come from a pure heart, uncontaminated by selfishness. Help me
to have the right motives and be genuinely and sincerely concerned
about other people's lives.

Empower My Life

Holy Spirit, I cannot live life on my own strength. I ask that You would
come and fill me with Your presence. Empower me with discernment
to make better life choices and energy to thrive—not just survive.
Give me a heart to seek You and serve others. Pour into my life more
love, joy, peace, and patience—to be a caring mom, a loving wife, a
good friend, a wise worker—a woman who is blessed, Lord.

Wounded Hearts

For I am poor and needy, and my heart is wounded within me.
PSALM 109:22 KJV

I hate being so needy, Lord, so poor, so hurt, so wounded. Troubles plague me on each and every side every time I try to depend upon myself to meet all my needs. Today I come to You, the source of all power. Grant me my petitions. Help me to rest assured that You are taking care of me and that as long as I abide in You, all will be well.

A Concentrated Focus

Lord, fatigue is the enemy of my faith. I refuse to grow weary in my walk with You. Help me to make You the center of all my activities. Give me a clear perception of my relationship with You so that I may learn Your ways and understand my place in Your plan. Like a beam of light breaks through the darkness, break through my mental fog, Lord, and teach me how to focus my attention on You.

Sharing My Blessings

*Every man shall give as he is able, according to the
blessing of the LORD your God which He has given you.*

DEUTERONOMY 16:17 NASB

Lord, You have blessed me and the works of my hands. I am so grateful to You for all that I have. As You bless me, I am able to bless others in whatever way I can. What a feeling to know that I am able to help expand Your kingdom! Help me to tithe my talents, monies, and time, all to Your glory. For thine is the kingdom and the power, forever and ever.

Knowing Your Worth and Value

Lord, I have sought to find my significance in places other than Your heart. Forgive me for putting weight in what other people think or in my own efforts. I thank You that You value me because I am Your child and that I have great worth no matter what I look like or do for a living. You find the unfading beauty of a gentle and quiet spirit to be of great worth in Your sight. Thank You for loving and valuing me, Lord.

Nothing Is Too Hard for God

*I am the Lord, the God of all mankind.
Is anything too hard for me?*

JEREMIAH 32:27 NIV

Lord, I want things to be different in my life—but there are so many obstacles. I need energy and motivation to get going. I need finances and more time. More than anything, I need to trust You more. Nothing is too difficult for You, Father. You can do anything! Despite all my needs and distractions, please bring into my life favor and openings. Please make a way. I ask that You would help me achieve the goals in my life that are best suited for Your good purposes.

A Worthy Life

*As a prisoner for the Lord, then, I urge you to live a
life worthy of the calling you have received.*

EPHESIANS 4:1 NIV

Lord Jesus, what an honor it is to be Your prisoner! I'm not locked up in jail as the apostle Paul often was, but I'm enslaved by love to You. You have called me to faith and to my vocation. I take them both seriously and want to live a life worthy of these callings. I thank You, Lord, that You empower me to do both.

Night and Day

*Now a true widow, a woman who is truly alone in
this world, has placed her hope in God. She prays
night and day, asking God for his help.*

1 TIMOTHY 5:5 NLT

Like the widow, Lord, I sometimes feel so alone, and so I put my trust in You. I come to You this morning, crying to You for help—financially, spiritually, emotionally, relationally, physically. I am in desperate need of You, my one and only source of hope! My hope today is on things unseen, remedies that You will bring to pass. As I rely on You, continue to feed my faith.

Self-Control

Lord, I need Your help. Please create in me the fruit of self-control—in all areas of my life. Empower me to walk in Your Spirit's power and to flee temptation. Help me to change the channel or walk away from the food or put my credit cards out of reach when I've been using them too much. Give me the strength I need to stay pure—both sexually and emotionally—around men to whom I am not married. Keep me, Lord, in the center of Your will.

Obedience and Blessings

All these blessings will come down on you and spread out beyond you because you have responded to the Voice of GOD, your God.

DEUTERONOMY 28:2 MSG

I hear Your voice, Lord, and I thank You for the blessings that You have showered upon me. Sometimes I feel so unworthy, but You love me so much that at times I cannot understand it. All that You have blessed me with goes beyond me, as I respond to Your voice, do Your will, and work to serve others. Speak to me, Lord. Tell me who, what, and where You want me to bless. I am Your servant, Lord; speak to me.

What Pleases God

How much more shall the blood of Christ, who through the eternal Spirit offered Himself without spot to God, cleanse your conscience from dead works to serve the living God?

HEBREWS 9:14 NKJV

God, I want to be passionate about the purpose You have for me. Show me the things in my life that please You, and give me the courage and strength to pursue those things. Keep my purpose before me, fill my heart, and give me right motives to accomplish all You have set before me. As long as You are with me and my focus is on what pleases You, I cannot fail.

Being a Person of Action

In the same way, faith by itself, if it is not accompanied by action, is dead.

JAMES 2:17 NIV

Lord, I want to be a person of action—a person of true faith. Faith by itself—if only thoughts and words—is dead. It has to be accompanied by my deeds, Lord. I pray for the wisdom to know when to take risks, when to act, and when to wait. Help me to know the right thing to do and the best time to do it. Put true faith into me, Lord, so I can perform the good works You have for me to accomplish.

Accountability

Lord, I pray for someone with whom I can share my inner life, someone who will hold me accountable. Please provide a mature woman who will mentor me and keep my life struggles confidential. I pray for someone with a loving heart—a person who won't judge me but will pray for and with me. Help me to be wise and responsible, but when I'm not, Lord, help me learn and grow in my spiritual development. I want to be strong in Your strength.

Well-Watered Gardens

*And the LORD shall guide thee continually, and satisfy thy soul
in drought, and make fat thy bones: and thou shalt be like a
watered garden, and like a spring of water, whose waters fail not.*

ISAIAH 58:11 KJV

You are the source of my life. Day by day You have met my needs in this sun-scorched land afflicted with the heat of greed and intolerance. As I come to You with today's petitions, may I be reminded of the ways You have rescued me in the past, resting in the assurance that You will once again deliver me from my troubles. Right now, in Your presence, I feel Your life springing up within me. Thank You for Your living water that never fails.

Standing Up for My Faith

*Let the message about Christ, in all its richness,
fill your lives. Teach and counsel each other with all
the wisdom he gives. Sing psalms and hymns and
spiritual songs to God with thankful hearts.*

COLOSSIANS 3:16 NLT

Heavenly Father, I want to let my light shine before all people. Teach me to live and act in a way that speaks Your truth to others. Fill me with an undying passion to see lives changed for Your glory. When I'm called to defend my faith, help me to do it in love, with gentleness and respect.

Daily Benefits

*Blessed be the Lord, who daily loads us with
benefits, the God of our salvation!*

PSALM 68:19 NKJV

I am loaded with benefits! Blessed beyond compare! You, the God of my salvation, the friend who laid down His life for me, the one who is with me in fire, flood, and famine, the one who will never leave me or forsake me! Today is a new day, and You have benefits waiting out there for me. I begin the day in my walk toward You, leaving my burdens behind and focusing on the benefits ahead. And when I come to You at the close of the day, You will be waiting for me at the end of the path with a good word.

Joy Despite Trials

Lord, it seems odd to consider trials a joyful thing. But I pray that my challenges in life, these times of testing, will lead me to greater perseverance. May that perseverance finish its work so I will be mature and complete, on my way to wholeness. I ask for wisdom and Your perspective as I seek joy in the hard times and the better times that will come my way.

Trusting God's Plans for My Life

*"For I know the plans I have for you," declares
the Lord, "plans to prosper you and not to harm
you, plans to give you hope and a future."*

JEREMIAH 29:11 NIV

Lord, You are the faithful God. I have hope for my future because of Your good promises. On You I rely. Reveal to me Your good plans for my life. As I share my dreams and visions with You, please mold them into reality—or mash them like clay on a potter's wheel into something more than I could ever have asked for or imagined. I put my trust in You, Lord.

Called According to His Purpose

*Who saved us and called us with a holy calling, not according
to our works, but according to His own purpose and grace
which was granted us in Christ Jesus from all eternity.*

2 TIMOTHY 1:9 NASB

Dear God, I thank You that our calling is not dependent upon our own efforts but upon Your purpose and the grace You gave us in Jesus. Your purpose is never random; it's something you've planned for all time. I want to be one with Your plan—one with You in Your eternal purpose of bringing people to know You.

Sharing Abundance

I needed clothes and you clothed me, I was sick and you looked after me, I was in prison and you came to visit me.

MATTHEW 25:36 NIV

Lord, as I present my needs to You and as You meet those needs, remind me of the needs of others, realizing that I may be *Your* answer to someone else's prayer today.

Real and Lasting Joy

Lord, I am so tired of imitations. People pretend to be something they're not. Food is flavored with artificial ingredients. It's hard to tell what is false and what is true anymore. When it comes to joy, I want the real thing. Pour into my life Your genuine and lasting joy. I need more of You, Lord. I pray for righteousness, peace, and joy in the Holy Spirit. Fill me, please.

The Law of Sowing and Reaping

Bring your full tithe to the Temple treasury so there will be ample provisions in my Temple. Test me in this and see if I don't open up heaven itself to you and pour out blessings beyond your wildest dreams.

MALACHI 3:10 MSG

Lord, Your Word says it is true—the more I give, the more I get. Yet that's not why I do it. I give of myself to bless others because that is what You have called me to do. The more I step out in Your Word, with You walking before me, the more I am blessed by Your presence and Your promises. It's not all about material things, although those are blessings as well. But I am more focused on the spiritual, for that is what keeps me close to You, unshaken, undisturbed, unfettered. Praise be Your holy name!

Our Real Calling

That you would walk worthy of God who calls you into His own kingdom and glory.

1 THESSALONIANS 2:12 NKJV

Dear Lord, this is my true calling: walking worthily into Your kingdom and glory. My vocational calling is but a reflection of Your highest priority. May I order my steps in such a way as to be worthy of Your calling, spiritually and professionally. Help me, Father, to show Your life within me to the world outside. May it be clear to those around me that You are the Lord of my life.

God Is Faithful

The one who calls you is faithful, and he will do it.
1 THESSALONIANS 5:24 NIV

Lord, I thank You that You are my faithful God. No one else is like You. People move away, jobs change, and much of life is uncertain. But You are always here, my stable, loving, and present Lord. Help me to hold unswervingly to the hope I profess, for You alone are faithful. You keep all Your promises—every one of them, all of the time—and I thank You for that, Lord.

Enjoying God's Blessings

Lord, I thank You for the work of Your hands. A wildflower, a mountain scene, the ocean waves on a white sand beach—the beauty of the earth reveals Your glory. Thank You for the smile of a child, the touch of my beloved's hand, the warmth of our home. I am grateful for the love of friends and meaningful work. You have done great things for us, and we are filled with joy. Thank You for Your many blessings.

Shouting for Joy!

Be glad in the LORD and rejoice, you righteous;
and shout for joy, all you upright in heart!

PSALM 32:11 NKJV

Your hands created the heavens and the earth. You breathed upon Adam and gave him life. Everything that was created was created through Your Son, Jesus Christ. The trees, the earth, the waters, and the creatures clap their hands in praise to You. This is the day that You have made! I will rejoice and be glad in it as I shout Your name to the heavens!

Waiting on God

I long, yes, I faint with longing to enter the courts
of the Lord. With my whole being, body and soul,
I will shout joyfully to the living God.

PSALM 84:2 NLT

My feet are positioned at the starting line. I'm ready to run the race. All I need now is Your signal for me to begin it. I believe I've found my passion and I'm ready to act on it, but I know I need to wait for Your timing. Help me to be patient. Alert me to what I still need to do in making my preparations.

Heavenly Blessings

All praise to God, the Father of our Lord Jesus Christ,
who has blessed us with every spiritual blessing in the
heavenly realms because we are united with Christ.

EPHESIANS 1:3 NLT

Because I am united with Your Son, who gave His life so that we could live, You have blessed me with every spiritual blessing. Here I sit, at my Savior's knee, His hand upon my head. I am at peace. I am blessed. I am in the heavenly realms. Here, nothing can harm me, for He has blessed me beyond measure. Lord, my cup runneth over with love for You!

Turning Sorrow to Joy

Lord, I give You my sorrow, and I ask for joy. I give You my pain, and I ask for healing. I give You my fears, and I ask for freedom and peace. Deliver me. Giver of good gifts, may I find a heart of gladness. In Your mercy and love, let me be a woman of courage, conviction, and confidence. Side by side, may I be in step with the Spirit as we journey through life together.

Surrendering Your Dreams

Going a little farther, he fell with his face to the ground and prayed, "My Father, if it is possible, may this cup be taken from me. Yet not as I will, but as you will."

MATTHEW 26:39 NIV

Lord, I humbly bow before You and give You my dreams. I give up control. I surrender my will for Yours. When I am tempted to do things my way, may I seek Your guidance instead. When I am too pushy, trying to make things happen on my own, give me mercy to see that Your grace has everything covered. I don't have to be afraid, Lord. I will trust You to meet my every need.

Finding Contentment

But godliness with contentment is great gain.

1 TIMOTHY 6:6 NIV

Lord, please help me to find my contentment in You. I don't want to be defined by "stuff"—the things I own or what I do. May my greatest happiness in life be knowing who You are and who I am in Christ. May I treasure the simple things in life, those things that bring me peace. With Your grace, I rest secure. Like Mary, I choose to sit at Your feet. You, Lord, are my satisfaction.

By His Great Mercy

In the morning, Lord, you hear my voice. . . . I,
by your great love. . .come into your house; in
reverence I bow down toward your holy temple.

PSALM 5:3, 7 NIV

Lord, I humble myself before You, bowing down at Your throne. You are so great, so awesome. Your presence fills this universe. I am filled with Your amazing love, touched by Your compassion. There is no one like You in my life, my Master, my Lord, my God.

Fear and Joy

Lord, fear is ugly and joy is beautiful. When fear is vanquished, joy becomes even more beautiful. So many people have a beautiful smile as they decide to follow You. They have replaced fear with the knowledge that they are following the one who sets aside all fear. I pray I will extinguish fear by remembering that I can put my trust in You.

Blessing Enemies

*Bless those who persecute you [who are cruel in their
attitude toward you]; bless and do not curse them.*

ROMANS 12:14 AMPC

God, I pray that you will bless those who have not been kind to me.
You know who they are. Give me the blessing of forgiving others as
You always forgive me. Help me not to repay evil with evil, but to
repay evil with good, for that is what You would have me do. Give me
the strength to be kind to them, even helpful, and to keep my anger
and frustration at bay. Bless their lives, Lord. In Jesus' name I pray.

The Peace That Brings Life

A heart at peace gives life to the body, but envy rots the bones.

PROVERBS 14:30 NIV

Lord, I thank You for the peace that restores me mentally, emotionally, and physically. It is the peace that brings wholeness. When
my heart is restless, my health suffers. But when I am at peace, You
restore my entire body. I can breathe easier, I can relax, and I can
smile again because I know everything's going to be all right. You
are in control. I thank You that Your peace brings life.

Patience for "in the Meantime"

Be patient, then, brothers and sisters, until the Lord's coming.
See how the farmer waits for the land to yield its valuable
crop, patiently waiting for the autumn and spring rains.

JAMES 5:7 NIV

Lord, it's hard to wait. There are so many things I want, and I'm inclined to charge ahead and "get it done." But You give us the "meantime" season for a reason. I ask for the patience and courage to wait well. Help me to be a woman of wisdom, knowing You have reasons for Your delays. You are not just killing time, Lord. You are ordering events and shaping my character. I yield to Your timing, Father.

Getting Stronger Every Day

Lord, my spouse and I have been through such trials, yet each time we make it over a hurdle together, our love grows stronger. What we had in the beginning of our marriage was good, but what we have now is better. Continue to help us through the trials of this life. Help us to keep a united front before our children. And in all things, may we praise Your name for the wonders and joy of marital love.

Praise Silences Enemies

*Through the praise of children and infants you
have established a stronghold against your
enemies, to silence the foe and the avenger.*

PSALM 8:2 NIV

With You on my side, You who hold the heavens in Your hands, You who sustain the entire universe, I need not be afraid of my enemies, of those who wish to harm me, or of the evil one who dogs my steps. With praises to You on my lips and in my heart, my foes are vanquished. You are my great refuge, my rock of strength.

Where Is Peace Found?

*For the kingdom of God is not a matter of eating and
drinking, but of righteousness, peace and joy in the Holy
Spirit, because anyone who serves Christ in this way is
pleasing to God and receives human approval.*

ROMANS 14:17–18 NIV

Lord, everyone is looking for peace. Some travel to other countries or try alternative philosophies and lifestyles to find an inner tranquility. Some think food or wine will satisfy the hole in the heart that only You can fill. But Your Word tells us it's not what we eat or drink that provides lasting satisfaction. May I find peace and joy in Your Holy Spirit, Lord. Knowing You, loving You, and experiencing You is true peace. Thank You, Lord.

A Daily Benediction

*The LORD bless you, and keep you; the LORD make His
face shine on you, and be gracious to you; the LORD lift
up His countenance on you, and give you peace.*

NUMBERS 6:24–26 NASB

May You walk down the road with me today. May You shower my path with Your many blessings. May You keep me from danger. May Your light keep me from the darkness surrounding me. May You give me grace and peace and strength for the day. May You give me someone to bless as You have blessed me. May You be there, waiting for me, at the end of the day, with a good word to calm my spirit as I rest in Your arms.

Lord, Change Me

Lord, look into my life and search my heart. Is there anything hurtful that I have been doing? Remove the sin and selfishness. Help me to stop focusing on how my spouse should change. Lord, cleanse *my* heart first. I can't change anyone else, so I ask You to show me what needs to go from my life, what needs to stay, and how I can be right with You. As You do, I pray for greater love and healing in our marriage.

To Know You, Lord

I want you to show love, not offer sacrifices. I want you to know me more than I want burnt offerings.

HOSEA 6:6 NLT

Heavenly Father, I am Your child. I belong to You. I want to know You more. Give me understanding of who You are and what You are like. Teach me the things that are important to You so they can become important to me. Help me to put You first in my life. Give me wisdom to choose time with You and to eliminate distractions that keep me too busy for You.

Peace with Others

Live in peace with each other.

1 THESSALONIANS 5:13 NIV

Lord, I need Your peace today. Some people are just hard to be around. They talk too much or seem too needy. Our personalities rub each other the wrong way. God, I need the power of Your Holy Spirit to stay calm. I don't want to be frustrated or lose my temper. I want to be at peace around others—even the people who so differ from me. Impart in me Your loving ways so I can be at peace with others.

His Awesome Power

Say to God, "How awesome are your deeds! So great is your power. . . . All the earth bows down to you; they sing praise to you, they sing the praises of your name."

PSALM 66:3–4 NIV

Lord, You parted the Red Sea. You stilled the wind and the waves. You gave sight to the blind and hearing to the deaf. You raised people from the dead. Your power is awesome. Nothing is impossible for You. I bow before You, singing praises to Your name.

Keep Us from Wandering

Lord, I ask in the name and power of Jesus that You would keep my husband and me from straying from our marriage vows. Keep our eyes from wandering and our hearts pure—toward you and toward each other—so that we never give in to an emotional or sexual intimacy outside our marriage. Help us not to discredit our union but rather to stay faithful and to cherish the special connecting bond we have with each other.

God, My Treasure

If riches increase, set not your heart on them.

PSALM 62:10 ESV

All the temporal things that now surround me will one day turn to ashes and dust. They mean nothing compared to the riches I find being with You. Although things are going well now, that may not be the situation tomorrow. Thus, I will not focus on what I have or do not have but on drawing ever closer to You, learning Your ways, and living the life You planned for me long ago.

Rest Assured

"Be still, and know that I am God; I will be exalted among the nations, I will be exalted in the earth."

PSALM 46:10 NIV

Lord, I thank You for the gift of Your peace and contentment in my life. You are awesome! I am learning that I can be at peace because You have a plan. You can handle anything—even my entire life. You are sovereign, powerful, and wise, and You never drop the ball. Because of who You are, I can be still and rest assured and confident no matter what comes my way. Thank You, Lord.

To Understand the Bible

You made me and formed me with your hands.
Give me understanding so I can learn your commands.

PSALM 119:73 NCV

The Bible is Your Word for my life. Help me to understand what You are saying to me through it. Give me wisdom and understanding as I allow scripture to feed my spirit and fill me with Your strength. I read Your words so I can grow and learn more about You. Bring the words I read back to mind when I need to apply them to the circumstances I face.

To Stay Connected

God, help me to stay connected to You throughout my day. I want to share it with You and be used by You to reach others. Speak to my heart, and remind me that You have something for me to do today. Lead me by Your Spirit.

Pleasing God Instead of People

Lord, help me to make friends with people who like me for me. Don't let me fall into the trap of trying to win friends by doing things that will entertain or please them. Give me courage when I find myself in the wrong crowd. Help me stay balanced in my friendships so I will always seek to please You rather than other people.

No Fear When God Is Near

*In God will I praise his word: in the LORD will I
praise his word. In God have I put my trust: I will
not be afraid what man can do unto me.*

PSALM 56:10–11 KJV

Your instruction keeps me on the right path, and for that I praise You.
Thank You for giving me Your Holy Word to have and to hold. With
Your Word, I can speak to You and You can speak to me. You are the
Great Communicator of my life. I trust in Your Word, for when I am
armed with it, I have no fear.

Letting Go of the Past

*My eyes are ever on the LORD, for only he will
release my feet from the snare.*

PSALM 25:15 NIV

Lord, it's hard to let go of things that are comfortable and familiar,
even when they're not good for me anymore. I need Your strong
power to release my grasp, finger by finger, on the things I cling to
so tightly—like unhealthy ways of thinking or relationships that are
not bearing fruit. As I release them to You, give me the courage to
receive all You have waiting for my empty, trusting hands.

Steady Work

*The one who stays on the job has food on the
table; the witless chase whims and fancies.*

PROVERBS 12:11 MSG

Lord, show me how to be content with my job. I know I need to work diligently so that I can provide for my family, but I am not sure that this is what You have called me to do. I feel trapped. Would chasing after my dream job be Your will for me, or is it just a whim? Lead me in the way I should go. Help me to be content in my present job and with the money I am earning. But if it be Your will, give me the courage to pursue the dreams You have for me.

For Boldness in Ministry

Lord, I don't know where to start in sharing my faith with others. When You give me the opportunity, help me to realize You are opening the door. Help me to recognize Your timing and to follow Your leading. Speak to me and through me. Give me Your words that will touch others' hearts and turn them toward a relationship with You.

Learn to Talk to Your Boss

*Trust in the Lord with all your heart;
do not depend on your own understanding.*

PROVERBS 3:5 NLT

Lord, thank You for my job and for giving me the support of my boss. Sometimes it can be intimidating to talk to my supervisor. I hate it when my mouth goes dry and my hands get sweaty. Fill me with Your confidence. Give me words to speak and the courage to say the things that need to be said. I was hired to do a job, and I will do it well because I know You are with me.

Learning from the Past

*Not only so, but we also glory in our sufferings,
because we know that suffering produces perseverance;
perseverance, character; and character, hope.*

ROMANS 5:3–4 NIV

Lord, I thank You for Your patience as I learn important lessons from my past. I don't want to repeat my mistakes, Lord. Your ways are not our ways, but Your ways are best. They bring healing and life. As I learn to rejoice in the suffering I've experienced, I can see Your hand teaching me perseverance; from perseverance, I develop character, and from character, I have hope.

Heart-Filled Praise

I will praise thee with my whole heart. . . . I will worship toward thy holy temple, and praise thy name for thy lovingkindness and for thy truth: for thou hast magnified thy word above all thy name.

PSALM 138:1–2 KJV

As I sit here before You, my heart reaches out to touch You, the great God, seated in the heavenlies. Meld my spirit with Yours so that our wills are one. Your love and faithfulness are tremendous. I praise You, Lord, with my lips, my voice, my mouth, my life.

When Others Are Watching

It's hard to be an example, Lord. I don't do everything the way I know I should. I want to be strong and diligent to do what is right. Help me hold fast to my convictions. Help me to be honest when I make mistakes. I want to encourage others by following You faithfully. Give me courage and strength to live my life to please You so I can say to them, "Follow me as I follow Christ."

The True Owner

"The earth and everything in it belong to the Lord."
1 CORINTHIANS 10:26 CEV

All I have is Yours. My spouse, my children, my parents, my car, my house, my furniture—everything is Yours. Whew! Somehow that takes a load off of my mind, knowing that I am merely Your steward. Give me the wisdom, Lord, to use the things of which you have given me temporary custody to further Your kingdom. I want to live my life to Your glory, not mine. Help me to do that today. Speak to my heart, I pray.

Moving Past My Mistakes

The thief comes only to steal and kill and destroy; I have come that they may have life, and have it to the full.
JOHN 10:10 NIV

God, You don't speak to me according to my past mistakes, and my heavenly rewards are not based on how many times I failed or succeeded. Although I can't erase my past, You can—and have. Thank You for removing my transgressions and filling me with Your great love and kindness in exchange. Help me to learn from my past and to move forward.

To Know the Truth

*We know also that the Son of God has come and has
given us understanding, so that we may know him who
is true. And we are in him who is true by being in his Son
Jesus Christ. He is the true God and eternal life.*

1 JOHN 5:20 NIV

Lord, thank You for making absolute truth available. You came into the world to testify for truth. It is not relative to what I think or feel. Truth is objective and is based on Your Word, the Bible. Help me to know the truth and see it clearly in my life.

Growing in Passion toward God

God, I am growing in faith as I get to know You better. I know You first by what You have done for me. You have saved me from darkness and transformed me. You have given me purpose and meaning. Thank You for reaching down and changing my life. I want to become passionate about the things that are important to You. Teach me what I need to know to complete the destiny You have given me. Time with You is a delight as I get to know and understand Your will for my life.

Lifelong Praise

*I will sing unto the L*ORD *as long as I live:*
I will sing praise to my God while I have my being.

PSALM 104:33 KJV

At this moment and throughout this day, I sing my praises to You, O God. Music is one of Your gifts, and I thank You for it. As my spirit in song rises to join with Yours, may I continually be reminded of all You are, all You have done, and all You will do.

Change Me, Lord

*Yet you, L*ORD*, are our Father. We are the clay,*
you are the potter; we are all the work of your hand.

ISAIAH 64:8 NIV

Lord, You know all about me—my past, my present, and my future. You are the potter and I am the clay, the work of Your hands. As You reshape my life, changing me from who I was and molding me into the woman You want me to be, help me to trust Your wisdom. I want to be a vessel sturdy enough to hold all the love You have for me—and to pour that out on others.

Truth Sets You Free

*To the Jews who had believed him, Jesus said, "If you hold
to my teaching, you are really my disciples. Then you
will know the truth, and the truth will set you free."*

JOHN 8:31–32 NIV

Lord, I am free! Finally! For so long I was bound in sin, selfishness, and unhealthy ways of thinking. I tried to change on my own, but like a prisoner in handcuffs, I was powerless; I could not break free on my own. Praise You, Lord—You loosed the chains that held me. Your love and strength empowered me, Lord. I choose to stay on Your path and follow the way of freedom. Your truth sets me free!

When God Seems Silent

God, forgive me for the times I walked away, too busy or self-absorbed to stay connected to You. I expect You to be upset with me, and I feel guilty, but Your love for me is unconditional. It's hard to trust when You are silent, but help me to do just that. And forgive me for the times when You were speaking and I wasn't listening. Help me to run to You instead of from You, so You can restore me to Yourself.

God and Emotions

*The Lord is slow to anger, abounding in love
and forgiving sin and rebellion.*

NUMBERS 14:18 NIV

Lord, what a blessing that You have given us such an array of emotions with which to express ourselves. Help me to be more like You—slow to anger and abounding in love. Help me to be a woman who is forgiving. I pray for more discernment, so that in whatever comes my way, I will have the grace to think, speak, and act with a good and godly attitude.

The Pursuit of Diligence

Lord, in all I do in pursuit of You, help me to be diligent. Help me to stay on task and accomplish my work faithfully and responsibly. No matter what work is set before me, I want to be motivated to do it as though I am doing it for You and not for others.

Praise for Forgiveness and Healing

Let all that I am praise the LORD; may I never forget the good things he does for me. He forgives all my sins and heals all my diseases.

PSALM 103:2–3 NLT

Dear Lord, You have given Your one and only Son to die for me. Because of You and Your great gift, I have eternal life. You have forgiven my sins and healed my soul. Nothing is impossible with You in my life. Thank You for taking care of me. With all that I am, with my entire being, I praise You forever and ever!

When I Feel Betrayed

It is no longer I who live, but Christ lives in me. So I live in this earthly body by trusting in the Son of God, who loved me and gave himself for me.

GALATIANS 2:20 NLT

Jesus, I know You experienced betrayal when Judas kissed You in the garden. What I am experiencing can't compare, but it brings me comfort knowing that You understand. I am hurt and feel so deceived. How can I open myself up and learn to trust someone again? Help me to heal quickly and forgive without compromising myself.

Don't Worry; Be Happy

For this reason I say to you, do not be worried about your life, as to what you will eat or what you will drink; nor for your body, as to what you will put on. . . . For your heavenly Father knows that you need all these things.

MATTHEW 6:25, 32 NASB

Your Word says I'm not to worry about my life, but that seems to be all that I do. I wonder how I'm going to pay all these bills. How did I get into such a mess? Get me back on the right track, Lord. Help me to get out of debt and stay out. Help me to not worry about where the next dollar is coming from but to put all my trust in You. You know all that I need. Please, Lord, provide for me and mine.

Fuel for My Passion

God, there is a fire burning in my soul to do what You have called me to do. Set things in motion to help me achieve the dream You gave me. Help me to hold tight to this passion and never let the fire in my soul burn out.

Renewing Your Mind

Do not conform to the pattern of this world, but be transformed by the renewing of your mind. Then you will be able to test and approve what God's will is—his good, pleasing and perfect will.

ROMANS 12:2 NIV

Lord, sometimes I feel like my emotions need a makeover. Renovate me—transform me so I can be balanced and healthy in my emotions. I ask for Your power to change. I don't want to be the way I used to be. I want to be wise and enjoy sound thinking. I want to make good decisions in how I express myself in my words and actions. Help me to know Your will and have a mind that's renewed.

When I'm Feeling Guilty

I will be merciful to their unrighteousness, and their sins and their lawless deeds I will remember no more.

HEBREWS 8:12 NKJV

Father, You gave me a fresh start when I received Your gift of salvation, but memories of my past sins find their way to the front of my mind. Remind me that You have wiped the slate clean. My past no longer exists for You. Relieve me of this pressure of guilt—my sin is gone! I let go of it today and refuse to let old memories enslave me. I give them all to You. Help me to create new memories of Your goodness and love for me. Thank You for setting me free.

Praise for Strength

O my strength, I will sing praises to You; For God is my stronghold, the God who shows me lovingkindness.

PSALM 59:17 NASB

When I am weak, Your strength upholds me. When I am afraid, Your courage sustains me. When I am downcast, Your presence lifts me. You are always there for me. How great, how wonderful, how amazing You are, my God, my Friend, my Father. I am here before You, singing endless praises to Your name!

Calm My Anxious Heart

Lord, I don't want to be anxious about anything, but so often I am. I thank You that You understand. Right now, I release my burdens and cares to You. I give You my heavy heart and my flailing emotions. I ask that You calm me, despite all that is happening in my life. As I keep my thoughts, actions, and attitudes centered on Jesus, Your peace comes. I thank You for Your peace that settles on me even when I do not understand.

Loyalty

"Is this your loyalty to your friend?
Why did you not go with your friend?"

2 SAMUEL 16:17 NASB

Lord, I want to be a better friend to those I love. Help me to be trustworthy, devoted, and reliable. Help me to put the desires of my friends before my own. Give me the power of encouragement so that I may be at their side with a ready word and a shoulder to lean on, with love in my heart and a prayer on my lips. I want to be like Jonathan was for David. I want to clothe others with the warmth of friendship. Make me a true friend. Who can I help today?

Keeping Promises to Myself

For we are each responsible for our own conduct.

GALATIANS 6:5 NLT

Lord, You created me for a specific purpose. I make promises to myself and think it's okay not to keep them. Help me to remember that I'm responsible to You for how my life turns out. Help me to keep the commitments I've set, and give me the courage to accomplish them. Remind me that it's okay to do good things for myself that help me to become the person You created me to be.

Love for Others

Dear friends, let us love one another, for love comes from God.
Everyone who loves has been born of God and knows God.

1 JOHN 4:7 NIV

Lord, You are the author of love. As I read Your Book and discover what love really is, help me receive it and express that love for others. Teach me Your ways. You are so good at loving people—You are kind, compassionate, interested, and accepting. You seek the best for other people. You empathize with their joy and sadness. You make them feel special. Lord, let me be a person who loves like that too.

The Wisdom of Peace

Lord, please plant Your wisdom in me like seeds in the soil. Help me cultivate each one and learn to follow Your ways. May I be a person who sows in peace and raises a harvest of righteousness. As I look to Your Word for growth, teach me to meditate on it and apply it to my life.

To Be a Better Friend

Father, help me to be sensitive to the people around me. Help me to prefer others to myself. I want to be a better listener so I really hear my friends. I want to help them if I can in the things that concern them. Let my words encourage them. Show me how to strengthen them with Your goodness.

Praise for the Father of Compassion

Blessed be the God and Father of our Lord Jesus Christ,
the Father of mercies and God of all comfort.

2 CORINTHIANS 1:3 NKJV

Lord, You love us so much. Fill me with that love to overflowing. Give me a compassionate heart. Lead me to the concern You would like me to champion for You, whether it be working in a soup kitchen, helping the homeless, or adopting a missionary couple. Lead me in prayer as I go down on my knees and intercede for others in distress.

When I Break a Promise

Good people will be guided by honesty; dishonesty
will destroy those who are not trustworthy.

PROVERBS 11:3 NCV

I did it again—I failed; I broke a promise. I feel guilty and ashamed. I thought I could pull it off, but I've hurt someone and disappointed myself and You. Forgive me for not counting the cost and thinking I could manage this alone. Give me the courage to apologize and correct my mistake, whatever it takes. Please comfort the people I hurt, and help them to forgive me and maybe let me try again.

Love One Another

[Jesus said], Love one another; as I have loved you.
JOHN 13:34 KJV

What an example of love You give us, Jesus! You laid down Your life for everyone even while we were still sinners. Fill me with that kind of love, Lord, that self-sacrificing love. So often, my thoughts seem to be all about me and what I want. Help me to change that by following Your example. I want to be like You, serving others with compassion, understanding, patience, and kindness. Give me that power, that longing, to love those who love me, those who hate me, and those who are indifferent to me.

Learning the Ways of Peace

Lord, I am so grateful that You are helping me become a person who walks in peace. Mentor me in Your ways so I can live in harmony and be a positive example for others. I don't want to put anyone down; I want to build them up. I don't want to start fights or nag people; I want to bring them happiness. Instead of putting myself first, let me be considerate of others. Forgive me if I have been proud or arrogant; teach me, Lord, to be humble.

Confidence

*Have no fear of sudden disaster or of the ruin that
overtakes the wicked, for the LORD will be at your side
and will keep your foot from being snared.*

PROVERBS 3:25–26 NIV

Lord, I want to be more confident. I don't want to be afraid of disasters—or just making mistakes. Give me the courage to know that You, Lord, will be my confidence. You keep me from tripping over my tongue and saying the wrong thing. But even when I do, You have the power to make things right again. Thank You for the confidence You give me. Let me walk with my head high because I know who I am in Christ: I am Yours!

Keeping Commitments to Friends

*You yourself must be an example to them by doing good
works of every kind. Let everything you do reflect the integrity
and seriousness of your teaching. Teach the truth so that
your teaching can't be criticized. Then those who oppose us
will be ashamed and have nothing bad to say about us.*

TITUS 2:7–8 NLT

I don't mean to take advantage of others, but I've done it. Forgive me for it. Jesus, open my eyes to see that I hurt my friends when I'm late, cancel, or just don't show up. Let me see this before it's too late to keep my commitments. Teach me how to schedule for interruptions and still keep the appointments that are most important on the schedule.

Intercession for World Leaders

*First of all, then, I urge that entreaties and prayers,
petitions and thanksgivings, be made on behalf of all men,
for kings and all who are in authority, so that we may lead
a tranquil and quiet life in all godliness and dignity.*

1 TIMOTHY 2:1–2 NASB

Dear God, today I lift up the world leaders—presidents, premiers, kings, queens, prime ministers, ambassadors to the United Nations, all rulers, princes, and governors. Give them wisdom, give them courage, give them minds of peace. There is so much death and destruction in this world, and at times I feel disheartened. But I know where to turn—to You, my Father, who makes all things right.

We Are Overcomers

Lord, our world is filled with trouble and pain—from the abuse, crime, and terrorism I see on the news to the drugs, affairs, and pornography addictions I hear about from people I know. Sometimes it seems like too much to handle. I am so glad that I have You, Lord. In this world there is trouble, but with You—being connected to You—I can have peace.

Turning the Other Cheek

The LORD restored the fortunes of Job when he prayed for his friends, and the LORD increased all that Job had twofold.

JOB 42:10 NASB

Job prayed for his friends even though they had argued with him and showed him their true colors. That's a true friend, Lord. And when he did this, You blessed him—giving him twice as much as he had before. That's amazing! That's the true power of forgiveness. You know the relationships I have with my friends. Sometimes it's hard to overlook the hurtful things they say and do. Help me to be more like Job—to learn to turn the other cheek and actually serve friends who disappoint me. I come to You this morning asking for that kind of compassion and dedication to my friends, Lord.

Prayer for Salvation

If you declare with your mouth, "Jesus is Lord," and believe in your heart that God raised him from the dead, you will be saved.

ROMANS 10:9 NIV

Lord, I humbly bow before You now and confess my sins to You. I am sorry for all of my wrongdoing, and I ask Your forgiveness. I believe Jesus is the Son of God and that He died on a cross and was raised from the dead. He conquered death so that I might really live—in power and purpose here on earth and forever with Him in heaven. I choose You. Please be my Savior and my Lord.

Compassion

Be kind and compassionate to one another,
forgiving each other, just as in Christ God forgave you.

EPHESIANS 4:32 NIV

Lord, Your compassion for people is great. You healed the blind, and You led the people who were lost like sheep without a shepherd. Create in me a heart of compassion—enlarge my vision so I see and help the poor, the sick, the people who don't know You, and the people whose concerns You lay upon my heart. Help me never to be so busy or self-absorbed that I overlook my family and friends who may need my assistance.

Returning to the Lord

Lord, some of the things in my past have led me far from You. I want to come back and be in right standing with You again. I ask for forgiveness for the things I have done wrong—in both my distant past and more recently. I am so glad that You are gracious and compassionate. Thank You for being slow to anger and abounding in love. Here I am, Lord, I return to You.

Reigning Peace

*[Jesus said,] These things I have spoken unto you, that in me
ye might have peace. In the world ye shall have tribulation:
but be of good cheer; I have overcome the world.*

JOHN 16:33 KJV

Dear God, how I pray for peace around the world. Some say it's impossible—but with You, all things are possible. And while peace may not yet reign throughout the earth, with You in my heart, peace reigns within for You have overcome the world! May all people feel Your peace within!

Thank You for Saving Me

Thanks be to God for his indescribable gift!

2 CORINTHIANS 9:15 NIV

Lord, I thank You for my salvation. I thank You for Your indescribable gift of eternal life and the power to do Your will today. I can hardly fathom how You suffered, yet You did it all for me—for every person on this planet. Mocked and beaten, You bled for my sins. You had victory over death so we could live. You made a way for me, and I am eternally grateful. Thank You, Lord.

Consistent Love

A friend loveth at all times.

PROVERBS 17:17 KJV

All I need is love! That's all I need from my friends right now. People who care about me, who want what's best for me, who will never turn away. But when I look at my past, I wonder if I've always loved my friends. I mean that constant, undying, unyielding love—the kind that You show for us. Forgive me, Lord, for the times I have fallen short. For times that I was so caught up in the busyness of my day that I did not show love to a friend who really needed it. Lord, fill me and my friends with Your love, and help us to let it flow freely to all we meet.

We Need to Remember

Lord, I want to remember the good things You have done for me in the past. Like the stones the Israelites took out of the Jordan River, I need my own personal "rocks of remembrance" of Your mercie in my life. You performed miracles for them—allowing them to cross the river on dry ground, parting the Red Sea for them—so that people today might know Your powerful hand. As I recall the ways You have helped me throughout my life, I honor You.

Needing Encouragement

May our Lord Jesus Christ himself and God our Father, who loved us and by his grace gave us eternal encouragement and good hope, encourage your hearts and strengthen you in every good deed and word.

2 THESSALONIANS 2:16–17 NIV

Lord, I need encouragement. Will You please inspire my heart and strengthen me in everything I say and do? I need Your truth to lift my spirit and help me soar. Let me be like an eagle that glides on the wind. Give me the courage and energy I need to keep going, even when I'm weary.

Power of the Cross

For the message of the cross is foolishness to those who are perishing, but to us who are being saved it is the power of God.

1 CORINTHIANS 1:18 NIV

Lord, I thank You for the wisdom to know the truth. People who do not know You think that the message of the cross—Jesus dying for the forgiveness of our sins—is foolishness. Truly, it is the power of God, and it saves us. Your power is amazing; there is no one like You. No one else can bring the dead back to life, perform miracles, and change lives like mine. Please help other people to know the power of the cross too.

Compassion for the Hungry

Is there any encouragement from belonging to Christ?
Any comfort from his love? Any fellowship together in the Spirit?
Are your hearts tender and compassionate? Then make me truly
happy by agreeing wholeheartedly with each other, loving one
another, and working together with one mind and purpose.

PHILIPPIANS 2:1–2 NLT

With the compassion You show to us, Your abiding tenderness through thick and thin, today I reach out to the hungry here and abroad. Open up my eyes to how I can help. Show me where my hands can be used to help feed those who are starving. I want to serve others in the name of Jesus Christ, for that is what You have called us to do. Open a door for me. Show me what I can do to make this world a better place.

Living in the Present

Lord, I have been camping in the past too long. Pull up my tent stakes, and help me to move on. There is so much to live for today! The past is over, and the future awaits. Today I choose to worship you, my Lord and Maker. When I hear Your voice, may my heart be soft—not hardened or jaded by the past. Today is a gift; I celebrate the present with You, Lord.

Weeping with Friends

*But first, please let me spend two months, wandering in
the hill country with my friends. We will cry together.*

JUDGES 11:37 CEV

Lord, my friend is in distress. She has lost something very dear to
her, and she has sunk down into the abyss. Give me the power of
encouragement so that I can help bear her burden. She has been
there for me so many times. Now I'd like to repay that kindness, that
love that she has given to me. Ease my schedule so that I can take
the time out of my day to give her words of comfort. Help me lift
her to You. All to Your glory, Lord!

Gift of the Holy Spirit

*You have made known to me the paths of life;
you will fill me with joy in your presence.*

ACTS 2:28 NIV

Lord, I have repented of my sins and asked You to come into my
life. I have received Your forgiveness. I thank You that Your Holy
Spirit now lives inside me. What a gift! I choose to acknowledge this
gift and ask that You would empower me to live a Spirit-filled life.
Let my thoughts and actions be full of life and light and love so
others may see Christ in me.

Stress

Cast your cares on the Lord and he will sustain you;
he will never let the righteous be shaken.

PSALM 55:22 NIV

Lord, I can't take one more day of this hectic whirl of life—the traffic, the crying kids, my workload at the office, and everything else I have to handle. Sometimes, it just feels like too much! Help me to breathe out my cares, casting them away like line from a fishing rod. But don't let me reel them back in! Here is my burned-out, anxious heart. May Your oceans of love and power replenish me, providing the energy I need to do what You want me to do each day.

Overcoming Oppression

Lord, I ask for Your strong power to heal me from oppression. I pray against evil and for good. I pray the shed blood of Jesus over my life. Keep me safe and protected. There is nothing, no single thing, that can keep me from you—neither death nor life, neither angels nor demons, neither the present nor the future, nor any powers, neither height nor depth, nor anything else in all creation. Cover me Lord, and be near me today.

Community Peace and Understanding

The weapons we fight with are not the weapons of the world.
On the contrary, they have divine power to demolish strongholds.

2 Corinthians 10:4 niv

God, through the divine power of Your Spirit and Your Word, I pray for my neighborhood. Demolish the stronghold of evil within this community. Touch each heart with Your peace and understanding. You know what each family needs. Help me to be an encouragement to them. Be with me as I take a prayer walk around this neighborhood, lifting each family up to Your heavenly throne.

Restored Relationships

Know that a person is not justified by the works of the
law, but by faith in Jesus Christ. So we, too, have put
our faith in Christ Jesus that we may be justified by
faith in Christ and not by the works of the law, because
by the works of the law no one will be justified.

Galatians 2:16 niv

Lord, You know how painful it is when things are not right between friends. I long for connected relationships, where people live in peace and harmony and there is no resentment between them. What a joy it is to know that I am made right with God by faith. We can communicate freely, talking and listening, enjoying each other as heart friends. I want to live in a growing love relationship with You. Thank You for restoration and righteousness.

New Friends

*If you fall, your friend can help you up. But if you fall
without having a friend nearby, you are really in trouble.*

ECCLESIASTES 4:10 CEV

Lord, there are people out there who are hard to love. Help me look beyond their cold demeanor, rudeness, shyness, and negative words and attitudes. You love each and every one of us and want us all to be friends. And if we were friends even to our enemies, the world would be at peace at last. No one deserves to be alone. Give me the courage and strength to reach out to all people and to make new friends.

Letting Go of Resentment

Lord, You know my feelings of resentment against certain people. Forgive me for feeling this way. I won't waste any more time or energy on this. I am only hurting myself by holding on to resentment. Help me to let go of the hurt and anger I feel. I don't want to hold grudges. I don't want this to have power over me any longer. I release them to You. You forgave me, and I choose to forgive them. I have no more desire for revenge. Help me to love them with the love You have shared with me.

Loneliness

Surely I am with you always, to the very end of the age.
MATTHEW 28:20 NIV

Lord, I thank You that You are my true companion—that I am never alone. You have assigned angels to watch over and protect me. You have given me your Holy Spirit and promised that You are with me always, even to the very end of the age. What a privilege that You call me Your friend. As we travel this road of life together, on city sidewalks, suburban roads, or country paths, I enjoy your presence, Lord. Help me never to forget Your presence.

God's Presence

"The virgin will conceive and give birth to a son, and they will call him Immanuel" (which means "God with us").
MATTHEW 1:23 NIV

Lord, I thank You for sending Your Son, God with Us, Emmanuel. Born of a virgin, You came to point us to the truth that saves us. You chose twelve disciples who followed You and learned the way to really live. You healed the sick; You gave sight to the blind. You were known for Your miracles and Your radical love for all kinds of people. Thank You for Your presence and that You live in me today.

Comfort for the Suffering

*[Jesus said,] "You are the light of the world—
like a city on a hilltop that cannot be hidden."*

MATTHEW 5:14 NLT

Dearest Christ, I pray for Your bright, shining light to spread out into the world. For Your love to reach the ends of the earth. Give comfort to those who suffer from abuse and violence. Touch them with Your healing light, and guard them with Your protective hand. Give them assurance that You are there. Allow them to feel Your presence, hear Your voice, feel Your touch.

When I've Compromised

Lord, thank You for showing me that the greatest danger to my faith can be when I'm tempted to compromise. Truth isn't negotiable, and I want to be on the side of truth. I don't want to compromise the character, nature, or values that come with my life in Christ. When I do, my old nature leads me instead of Your spirit. Forgive me and help me to stay the course. Guide me in Your truth so I can stand strong, unwilling to compromise.

Building Blocks

So encourage each other and build each other
up, just as you are already doing.

1 Thessalonians 5:11 nlt

Lord, I want to be a Barnabas—an encourager. I want to build people up, block by block, and not tear them down. Words can be so painful, so wrenching to the soul, heart, spirit, and confidence of others. Help me to be an encourager to others. Put a kind word in my mouth. And as I do so, may others continue to encourage me, especially those at church. Sometimes, even there, we get our feelings hurt. Help me to be Your representative inside and outside of the body of believers. Give me words that are sweet to the soul!

Let's Grow

Like newborn babies, crave pure spiritual milk,
so that by it you may grow up in your salvation.

1 Peter 2:2 niv

Lord, I want to grow up spiritually. I want to transition from a newborn baby who drinks only milk to a more mature believer who craves the "meat" of deeper things. I want to move from head knowledge to heart experience with You. I want to know what it means to enjoy Your presence, not just to make requests. Step by step and day by day, teach me to follow and learn Your ways.

Anger

*Get rid of all bitterness, rage and anger, brawling
and slander, along with every form of malice.*

EPHESIANS 4:31 NIV

Lord, I am so mad! I am angry, and I need Your help. Why do things have to go so wrong? I need to do something with this emotion—and I choose to give You my anger and bitterness, Lord. Help me be rid of it. Redeem the confusion, and bring peace to what seems so out of control. Free me from resentment and blame. Show me my part in this conflict as you speak to the heart of my nemesis. I need your healing and peace, Lord.

The Ultimate Gift

Lord, thank You for the greatest gift—forgiveness. I am honored to be a recipient of Your mercy. It's a gift I want to share with others. Help me to learn to forgive others easily. You are my example. When I'm tempted to react to the things that hurt and offend me, remind me of Your willingness to forgive me. Teach me to see things from others' perspectives. Give me a heart of compassion so I freely give others the ultimate gift that You have shared with me.

Change the Hearts of Terrorists

*Finally, all of you, be like-minded, be sympathetic,
love one another, be compassionate and humble.*

1 PETER 3:8 NIV

Dear Lord, please soften the calloused hearts of those who deem themselves terrorists. Exchange their hearts of stone for ones tender with love. Protect the innocent here and abroad, especially missionaries who risk their lives to spread Your light. Comfort those who have lost loved ones through the violence around the world. Lord, can't we all just get along?

I Will Follow You

*Then he said to them all: "Whoever wants to be my disciple
must deny themselves and take up their cross daily and
follow me. For whoever wants to save their life will lose
it, but whoever loses their life for me will save it."*

LUKE 9:23–24 NIV

Lord, here I am before You. I am ready to "take up my cross" and follow You. Every day, I want to be with You, empowered by You, and loved so deeply that I am changed. Show me what it means to lose my life in order to save it. Teach me about surrender, knowing You lift me up to do Your good purposes. Transform me, Lord. Teach me to follow You.

On Eagles' Wings

I carried you on eagles' wings and brought you to myself.
Exodus 19:4 NIV

God, I need You to lift me up, above all these problems, above my circumstances, above my helplessness. Carry me off to Your place in the heavenlies, where I can find my breath, where I can sit with You, where I can find the peace of Your presence. You alone can carry me through this. I feel myself drifting off, Your strong arms holding me close, Your breath touching my face. Thank You, Lord, for saving my soul. My spirit rejoices!

When I've Judged Others

Jesus, please forgive me for judging others. I hate it when others judge me, but it's so easy to condemn, categorize, and criticize the choices others make. Forgive me for being close-minded, opinionated, self-righteous, and unloving toward the very people You gave Your life for. They are valuable and precious to You. Teach me to see them that way too. Help me to allow others to express their thoughts and opinions without feeling that my own beliefs are under attack. It is not my place to judge anyone. If possible, let me bring them Your truth in love.

Healing Guilt and Shame

For day and night your hand was heavy on me; my strength was sapped as in the heat of summer. Then I acknowledged my sin to you and did not cover up my iniquity. I said, "I will confess my transgressions to the Lord." And you forgave the guilt of my sin. Therefore let all the faithful pray to you while you may be found; surely the rising of the mighty waters will not reach them.

PSALM 32:4–6 NIV

Lord, my shame makes me want to hide. But I can no longer hide in the darkness of my guilt and sin. You already know everything I've done wrong, yet you bring me into the light—not to condemn nor to condone but to heal me. I acknowledge my wrongs and confess them all to You, Lord. I stand in Your forgiveness as the cleansing water of Your gentle love flows over me, washing away my guilt and shame.

The First Priority

Love the Lord your God with all your heart and with all your soul and with all your mind. This is the first and greatest commandment.

MATTHEW 22:37–38 NIV

Father, You are my everything! Without You, I wouldn't even be here. Forgive me for allowing so many other things to squeeze between me and You. Help me to become more diligent in my time with You. It fills me with the strength I need to make it day after day. I love You so much! I never want to take our relationship for granted.

Victory for Youth

For our struggle is not against flesh and blood, but against the rulers, against the powers, against the world forces of this darkness, against the spiritual forces of wickedness in the heavenly places.

EPHESIANS 6:12 NASB

Lord, I pray that You would oust the unseen evils from this land, that Your angels would battle fiercely against the dark forces corrupting our youth. Empower our youth leaders to claim a victory for young hearts. Show me how I can help at my church, how I can lead teens to You. Give parents the right words to say when dealing with their children.

Easily Offended

Lord, I have such anger within me for all the wrongs done to me all day long. Even when I'm out in traffic and someone cuts me off, I'm really miffed. Or when my family comes to the dinner table and no one appreciates how hard I've worked to make this meal but complains about every little thing, I just want to scream! Give me that new heart. Empty this heart of stone, the one so easily offended. Fill it with Your love.

Emergency Call

A hostile world! I called to God, to my God I cried out.
From his palace he heard me call; my cry brought me
right into his presence—a private audience!

2 SAMUEL 22:7 MSG

This trial, this thing I'm going through, Lord, I don't know how to handle it. I don't know what to do. But I am certain of one thing and one thing only: You can handle it. You hear me when I cry out to You, and You bring me directly into Your presence. You are ready to listen to me, to my groanings and my pleas. Help me, Lord, to find the strength to carry on.

Living in the Now

And the second [greatest commandment] is like it:
"Love your neighbor as yourself."

MATTHEW 22:39 NIV

I can't change the past, but I think about it a lot. It's a waste of time, and I hate for my mind to go there. I don't want to recount my past mistakes—I've been forgiven. Lord, help me to focus on today. Help me to keep my attention on the priorities You have given me. Help me to live in the present. Show me what I can do today to make an eternal difference.

Sadness

Why, my soul, are you downcast? Why so disturbed within me? Put your hope in God, for I will yet praise him.

PSALM 42:5 NIV

Lord, I feel so gloomy today. Do you see my tears? In my sadness, help me to remember that even when I'm down, I can choose to put my hope in You. Instead of telling myself lies that push me deeper into despair, I can look to Your truth. Remind me of the good things You have done in the past. I choose to praise You. You are my Savior and my God. May Your love comfort me now.

Forgive and Forget

Why can't I forgive and forget, Lord? Please help me forgive the person who injured me the other day. Instill in me Your power, Your grace, and Your mercy. With each breath I take in Your presence, I feel that power growing within me. Thank You, Lord. Now, please give me the means to forget this pain. I don't want to keep bringing it up and picking at the wound. Help me, Lord, as weak as I am, to forgive the offender and forget the pain.

Protection for Missionaries and Pastors

"If it be so, our God whom we serve is able to deliver us from the furnace of blazing fire; and He will deliver us."

DANIEL 3:17 NASB

I pray for others with the confidence that You, dear Lord, hear my prayer. That although at times this world seems so unsettled, Your hand is upon our missionaries and pastors, guarding them when they are awake and as they sleep. Give them the strength to do what You have called them to do. Give them the means to help the lost, starving, diseased, and imprisoned. Give them wisdom as they reveal Your Word and reach into the darkness to spread Your light.

When Others Fail Me

Make allowance for each other's faults, and forgive anyone who offends you. Remember, the Lord forgave you, so you must forgive others.

COLOSSIANS 3:13 NLT

When others fail me, it makes me feel unimportant to them. It hurts my feelings, and I want to be angry. Remind me of the times when circumstances were out of my control and I missed a commitment and failed someone. Fill me with compassion and understanding for their situation. Help me to get over it and show them Your love.

Needing Direction

*Thus says the LORD: "Stand in the ways and see, and
ask for the old paths, where the good way is, and walk
in it; then you will find rest for your souls."*

JEREMIAH 6:16 NKJV

Lord, I come before You, standing here, seeking Your face. I need direction. I feel so lost, so alone. But You are here with me, to lead and guide me, to show me the way I should go. With You and You alone, I can find rest for my soul. Give me the peace of Jesus. Peace like a river. Peace. . . Peace. . . Peace. . . Lord, give me peace.

Holding That Tongue

Whenever I bring up past deeds, I start the cycle of pain all over again. Why do I do that, Lord? Please stop me! Help me to hold my tongue, to think before I speak. Change my thoughts to those of Christ. Help me to think of the good things, the good times, I have shared with my offenders. And if there weren't any good times, remind me that You love them just as much as You love me. Help me to put their need for forgiveness above my pride. Give me Your power to live this life and be the person You want me to be.

Depression

He lifted me out of the slimy pit, out of the mud and mire;
he set my feet on a rock and gave me a firm place to stand.
He put a new song in my mouth, a hymn of praise to our God.
Many will see and fear the Lord and put their trust in him.

PSALM 40:2–3 NIV

Lord, will you please change the music of my life from a sad, minor key to a joy-filled, major key? Give me a new song to sing, a happier tune! It's amazing to me that there is no mess too big for You to fix, no broken life too shattered for You to restore, and no loss too great for You to redeem. As You raise me out of the darkness of my slimy pit, lifting me from the mud and mire of my depression to solid emotional ground, I will praise You.

Responding Well to Criticism

Fools show their annoyance at once, but the prudent
overlook an insult. An honest witness tells the truth, but
a false witness tells lies. The words of the reckless pierce
like swords, but the tongue of the wise brings healing.

PROVERBS 12:16–18 NIV

Lord, I don't like being criticized. I ask for a calm spirit when others make cutting remarks. Please give me insight to know if what is said is true and if I need to make changes in my life. If not, Lord, I ask You to heal my heart from these verbal barbs. Please give me patience and discernment to keep my cool and not lash out in retaliation. Please bring our relationship through this criticism.

Message of Eternal Life

The world and its desires pass away, but whoever
does the will of God lives forever.

1 JOHN 2:17 NIV

The world may pass away, but Your love never fails. Those who believe in You will live with You forever. What a blessed thing! I pray that others around the world will hear the message so that they too can accept Your gift of eternal life. Show me how I can help spread the message, all to Your glory.

Trusting God with Changes

Help me to be willing to step out of my comfort zone to go where You want me to be. I want to remain focused on Your purpose for me, never looking back but pressing forward in my journey with You. Show me how to lean on You when I feel out of place or alone. I know You are always with me.

Lifted Out of the Pit

"Do not fear, for I am with you; do not anxiously look about you, for I am your God. I will strengthen you, surely I will help you, surely I will uphold you with My righteous right hand."

ISAIAH 41:10 NASB

I am in such turmoil. I don't understand what's happening or why. All I know is that I am stressed out, and I can't seem to get a handle on anything anymore. Lift me up out of this pit, Lord. I trust in You. I know that You can uphold me, that You can help me rise above the troubles of this world for You have overcome this world. I know that I am precious in Your sight and that You will not allow evil to harm me. Save me, lift me, meet me now!

Blessings from the Work of Your Hands

The Lord your God will bless you in all your harvest and in all the work of your hands, and your joy will be complete.

DEUTERONOMY 16:15 NIV

Lord, I ask that You would bless the work of my hands. As I sit at a computer or fold laundry or teach a classroom of children, may my work be meaningful and bear good fruit. I pray for a spirit of joy during the day as I go about my business. I pray for a cheerful countenance and a willing, servant's heart. I dedicate my work life to You, Lord, for Your good purposes and blessings.

Praise for God's Indescribable Gift

For God so loved the world that he gave his one and only Son, that whoever believes in him shall not perish but have eternal life.

JOHN 3:16 NIV

Thank You for giving the most precious gift, Your very own Son, so I could live each day with You. There are no words to describe the depths of Your sacrifice, but I know You did it for me. You gave Your first and only Son so You could share life with many sons and daughters. I am so thankful Jesus was willing to give His life for mine.

Personal Responsibility

Lord, give me a sense of personal responsibility for the lost. Teach me ways I can bless others. Strengthen my decision to lead others to You. May I progress from my home to my neighbors to my extended family. Almighty God, I surrender myself to Your service.

A Firmly Founded Friendship

Lord, help me to establish a firm foundation of loyalty, trust, honesty, and integrity in my friendships. When our eyes are on You, we will remain strong in our commitment to You and to one another. Help me to discern when I need to drop a task and be there for my friends.

Clothed with Compassion

*Therefore, as God's chosen people, holy and
dearly loved, clothe yourselves with compassion,
kindness, humility, gentleness and patience.*

COLOSSIANS 3:12 NIV

As I get down on my knees, I wrap myself within the cloak of compassion. I bring to You specific concerns for which You have led me to pray, knowing that You hear my prayer, confident that You will answer. And as I rise from the place of prayer, may Your kindness, humility, gentleness, and patience shine through me and lighten the hearts of others. I want to be Your servant. Help me to change the world.

Reducing Stress

*Do not be anxious about anything, but in every situation, by prayer
and petition, with thanksgiving, present your requests to God.*

PHILIPPIANS 4:6 NIV

Lord, I have so much to do—please help me! Deadlines and details swirl around me like a swarm of bees. I feel heavy pressure with my heavy workload. Help me to do what needs to be done each day so I can stop worrying and rest well at night. I give You my anxiety and stress—I release it all to You, Lord. As Your peace covers me, the peace that passes all understanding, may it guard my heart and mind in Christ Jesus. I rest in the comfort of Your love.

True Colors

Consider it a sheer gift, friends, when tests and challenges come at you from all sides. You know that under pressure, your faith-life is forced into the open and shows its true colors. So don't try to get out of anything prematurely. Let it do its work so you become mature and well-developed, not deficient in any way.

JAMES 1:2–4 MSG

Lord, I haven't been handling the stress very well lately. How do I let myself get into these situations? I know I am to consider it a challenge when I am under pressure, but right now I feel like I'm challenged out. Help me to find joy in the journey, Lord. To remember that no matter what happens, You are on this ride with me. May the pressure that is on me now make me more like Christ. But at the same time, Lord, give me peace!

When I'm Tempted to Take Shortcuts

God, people around me take moral shortcuts, but I know that isn't right for me. You have given me values of honor, integrity, and truth. Help me not to compromise. Although others may act without integrity as they climb the corporate ladder, it's not worth the price of my relationship with You to follow their example. You bless me because I choose what is right and just. Thank You for reminding me of the way I need to go.

Take Up Your Cross

*Then he said to the crowd, "If any of you wants to
be my follower, you must give up your own way,
take up your cross daily, and follow me."*

LUKE 9:23 NLT

Jesus, it takes sacrifice to follow You. I have so many dreams for my life, but they are nothing unless they include You. Help me to let go of the things I selfishly desire and that aren't meant to be a part of my life. Your purposes for my life mean success. I give You my life—I completely surrender.

Balancing Work and Life

*Am I now trying to win the approval of human beings, or of
God? Or am I trying to please people? If I were still trying
to please people, I would not be a servant of Christ.*

GALATIANS 1:10 NIV

Lord, every day is a juggling act with work, my home, my spouse, kids, ministry, and friends. I rarely have time for myself—just to be with You or even to remember who I am. Teach me to center on You, Lord, and keep my focus. I can't please everyone, and really, You've never asked me to. You are the one I seek to please. Be the hub of my heart, the steady center that moves the wheel of my life forward.

Home, School, and Streets

You are of God, little children, and have overcome them,
because He who is in you is greater than he who is in the world.

1 JOHN 4:4 NKJV

Lord, there are so many dark forces within our schools, on the streets, and even in our homes. I pray for Your light to eliminate the evil among us. I know that no matter what, You will prevail, dear Jesus. You have overcome this world. You have the power to do the impossible. Show me how I can make this world a better place. Give me the heart to intercede for others and the courage to step in when and where I am needed.

Be Content

I am not saying this because I am in need, for I have learned
to be content whatever the circumstances. I know what it is to
be in need, and I know what it is to have plenty. I have learned
the secret of being content in any and every situation, whether
well fed or hungry, whether living in plenty or in want.

PHILIPPIANS 4:11–12 NIV

Lord, I often think about what could be and dream of a better future. Sometimes, though, my thoughts are locked in the past, stuck in disappointment and regret. Please help me to be content with today, to live in this moment, no matter what my current circumstances. In every situation, may I look to You for peace. Still the storms in my heart so that whether I am at rest or in motion, I can find Your serenity and strength.

Blessings Amid the Storm

I said to myself, "Relax and rest. God has showered you with blessings."

PSALM 116:7 MSG

Lord, when I look back on all the ways You have blessed me and continue to bless me, even through these trials, I am awed and thankful. As You have delivered me in the past, deliver me again from the troubles before me. Lift the burdens off my sagging shoulders. I leave them at the foot of Your cross, as instructed. Thank You, Lord. I love You so much. Now with each breath I take, I relax and enter into Your rest.

Chosen to Serve

Father, at an assembly of the church, I expect to be renewed, strengthened, and aligned with Your will. I understand that to reach those goals, I must assist others and accept those assignments for which I've been chosen to serve. Often, Lord, I can find excuses for avoiding my obligations. Help me understand that when I neglect these opportunities to serve, I'm also neglecting my spiritual growth.

Asking for God's Help

God is my helper; the Lord is with those who uphold my life.
PSALM 54:4 NKJV

Sometimes I feel You have so much on Your plate that I should work things out on my own. I know I shouldn't feel like I'm bothering You, but my problems seem small compared to what others deal with. Still, I know You want to help me. You are just waiting for me to ask, so I'm asking—please, help. You know what I'm dealing with. Forgive me for not coming to You sooner. I accept Your help today.

Who's the Boss?

*In God I trust and am not afraid. What can man
do to me? I am under vows to you, my God;
I will present my thank offerings to you.*
PSALM 56:11–12 NIV

Lord, I pray for a right mind-set with the person for whom I work. Help me to submit to her authority and work with honesty and integrity. Yet, while I report to someone in my occupation, may I have the firm conviction that You are my highest authority. My ultimate trust is in You, Lord, not in any man or woman. As I report to You each day for guidance, help me to serve You well.

Finding Your Gift

*Don't act thoughtlessly, but understand
what the Lord wants you to do.*

EPHESIANS 5:17 NLT

Lord, I'm looking for direction. I'm not sure how You want me to serve You. So many times I feel so inadequate, that others can do things better than I ever could. But I know those feelings are not of You. Help me to understand, Lord, how You want me to serve, what You want me to do. Not worrying about pleasing others but pleasing You, I will do so all to Your glory.

May Christ Dwell in Your Hearts

In him and through faith in him we may approach God with freedom and confidence. I ask you, therefore, not to be discouraged because of my sufferings for you, which are your glory. For this reason I kneel before the Father, from whom every family in heaven and on earth derives its name. I pray that out of his glorious riches he may strengthen you with power through his Spirit in your inner being, so that Christ may dwell in your hearts through faith (Ephesians 3:12–17 NIV).

The Secret Joy in Jesus

*He who dwells in the secret place of the Most High
shall remain stable and fixed under the shadow of the
Almighty [Whose power no foe can withstand].*

PSALM 91:1 AMPC

I come to You today, meeting You in that secret place where I know I am safe. You are my rock, my sure foundation. Hiding in You, I will come to no harm. I rest in this place, seeking Your face. Jesus, Jesus, Jesus. There is magic in that name. There is peace in this place. There is love in Your eyes. I praise Your holy name! I smile in Your presence. You are the joy of my life!

Find Success

*Commit to the Lord whatever you do,
and he will establish your plans.*

PROVERBS 16:3 NIV

Lord, I ask for success and favor for all I put my hands to today. Bless my work, please. May the time and effort I put into it bear abundant fruit. I commit my plans to You, Lord, and surrender my will for Yours. In all I seek to accomplish, in all I hope to become as a woman of God, may my plans succeed. I pray for victory and triumph as You reveal to me what true success should look like in my life.

Experiencing God's Strength

God is my strength and power, and He makes my way perfect.
2 SAMUEL 22:33 NKJV

Life's demands seem heavier than ever before. I am taking a moment right now to recharge my soul with Your strength. Remind me that my help comes from You—whatever I need. You are my power source, and I plug in right now. Fill me up physically, mentally, and emotionally. Thank You that I don't have to go through my life alone. You are always there to recharge me when my power supply is running low. I rest in You today.

Not Ashamed

Lord, I am not ashamed of the Gospel. Your words have the power to bring salvation to every person who believes. I don't want to hide the light of truth, but instead to let it shine from my life so others will see Christ in me. When people ask me about the source of my joy, give me the words to share so they can know You too. Help me bring glory to You as I stand with courage and strength in the truth.

Serving from the Heart

As slaves of Christ, do the will of God with all your heart.

EPHESIANS 6:6 NLT

I want to work for You, Lord, using all my heart, soul, and talent. I want to be Your tool, serving You with passion. And as I do so, help me to keep my eye and focus on You and not on the gift You have given me. Help me to understand what You have shaped me to do.

A Heart to Serve

*The Lord is gracious and compassionate,
slow to anger and rich in love.*

PSALM 145:8 NIV

Lord, I pray for a spirit of compassion. Help me to care about the needs of others and have genuine love for the ones I serve. Pour into me Your caring, kind spirit so I can be a blessing and minister out of a full heart. Fill me to overflowing so my ministry will be effective, growing, and blessed. May I walk in Your graciousness with a heart to serve.

Unceasing Prayer

Prayer was made without ceasing of the church unto God for him.
ACTS 12:5 KJV

God, I remember how Peter's friends prayed for him while he was in prison, how they constantly and consistently interceded for him. You sent an angel to visit Peter, and his chains fell off! Help me to be such a prayer warrior today. Lord, tell me whom to pray for this morning. And may such deliverance come to that person according to Your will.

Overwhelmed

God, I have so many things to do today. I feel overwhelmed. But I am here to be Your hands and feet. You have known since the beginning of time what I am to accomplish each and every day. Give me the wisdom to do what You want me to do, to be the person You want me to be.

No Doubt

*But when you ask, you must believe and not
doubt, because the one who doubts is like a wave
of the sea, blown and tossed by the wind.*

JAMES 1:6 NIV

Lord, rescue me from my sea of doubt and fear. I have lived with uncertainty and suspicion for too long. I don't want to be like an ocean wave that is blown and tossed by the wind. I ask that You would quiet my stormy emotions and help me believe that You will take care of me. When I'm tempted to be cynical, help me choose to step away from fear and closer to faith.

Provision and Resources

*The next day we landed at Sidon; and Julius,
in kindness to Paul, allowed him to go to his
friends so they might provide for his needs.*

ACTS 27:3 NIV

Lord, Your resources are unlimited. You delight to give Your children good gifts, to meet their needs. I boldly and humbly ask that You would provide for the needs of my ministry. Bring our ministry to the minds of people who are willing to give out of their God-given resources. May they give of their time, money, talents, or other resources to bless these ministry efforts to further Your kingdom.

Created for Good Works

We are God's masterpiece. He has created us anew in Christ
Jesus, so we can do the good things he planned for us long ago.

EPHESIANS 2:10 NLT

You have shaped me into the unique person I am today. You have created me to do good works. I am awed that You prepared things in advance for me to do. From the very beginning, You made me for a specific job in Your kingdom. Give me the courage to take hold of that task. Help me not to shy away from the challenges that face me.

Let It Be

I acknowledge that You are in control of everything, Lord, and that the things You want me to accomplish today will get done. I want to walk in Your will and not in mine. I want to lean on Your Word and take Your paths. I can only do that by putting my total trust in You as I go through this day. I want to be like Mary. I want to be Your servant, saying, "Let it be to me according to your word" (Luke 1:38 NKJV). So, Lord, help me to accomplish what You want me to do today, and let the rest be.

Jesus in Our Midst

For where two or three are gathered together in
my name, there am I in the midst of them.

MATTHEW 18:20 KJV

Lord, it's amazing that when we come together with other believers—even when just two believers are together—You show up! You are in the midst of us! You love us that much. Be with Your body of believers today, Lord, whenever and wherever they are meeting around the world. Show them Your power, Your presence. Answer their prayers today, Lord. All to Your glory!

For the Poor and Needy

When you give to the needy, do not let your left
hand know what your right hand is doing, so that
your giving may be in secret. Then your Father, who
sees what is done in secret, will reward you.

MATTHEW 6:3–4 NIV

Lord, I pray today for the poor and needy. Many need money, while others are poor in spirit. Please provide food and water to meet their physical needs and the gospel of Jesus Christ and His saving love to fill their souls. Lord, show me how I can be part of the solution. Show me where I can give and serve. Use my abilities and finances to help, for Your glory.

Safe in Danger

For in the day of trouble he will keep me safe in his dwelling; he will hide me in the shelter of his sacred tent and set me high upon a rock.

PSALM 27:5 NIV

Lord, I need Your protection. Keep me safe in your dwelling place. Hide me from my enemies in your secure shelter. Comfort me with Your warm blanket of peace and love. I am safe with You, and in Your protection—in Your presence—I can move from fearful to fearless, from timid to trusting. Here, Lord, I am safe from harm.

Capturing Thoughts

God, it seems like I need a reminder every moment of the day to listen to Your voice. I keep getting caught up in the world of busyness, and that's not where You want me to be. Help me not to be overwhelmed by the demands of this society but to be open to Your voice. I want to hear You speak to me all throughout the day. I want to do only what You want me to do each moment. Remind me to take each thought captive to Christ so that I am not misled, going somewhere or doing something that is not of You.

Different Gifts, Same God

There are different kinds of gifts, but the same Spirit distributes them. There are different kinds of service, but the same Lord. There are different kinds of working, but in all of them and in everyone it is the same God at work.

1 CORINTHIANS 12:4–6 NIV

Give me the humility You had when You washed the feet of the disciples. I am willing to take on whatever task—high or low—that You have for me. Grant me the spirit of cooperation as I work with others. Show me how to use my gift in new and different ways. I serve to bring glory and honor and blessing to You.

For Those in Prison

I was in prison and you came to visit me.

MATTHEW 25:36 NIV

Lord, I pray for the men and women in prison all over our country today. I ask for a revival—that many would come to know You, love You, and serve You. Help those who are incarcerated to know that You are the one who sets people free from the bondage of sin and wrongdoing. Help them to know that only You offer a life of hope and peace. In the darkness, help them to find Christ's forgiveness, joy, and light. Remind my heart, Lord, to visit those in prison and fulfill Your commands.

Testimony of Believers

*They were heartily welcomed by the church and
the apostles and the elders, and they told them all
that God had accomplished through them.*

ACTS 15:4 AMPC

Lord, when I hear what other people say You have done in their lives, their testimonies buoy my own faith. It gives me chills when I hear of the wonders of Your deeds. Give me the courage to share my testimony with others, knowing this will draw unbelievers to You and strengthen the hearts of those who already know You. Thank You, Lord, for hearing my prayer.

Lead Me by the Hand

Here we go, Lord—another morning with a thousand things to do. Lead me by the hand, for I don't know which way to go. I have trouble with my priorities, Lord. The only thing I seem to be able to remember is that You are first in all things. So here I am, seeking You first. Plan my day as You see fit. Direct my steps to walk Your path. Life can get so complicated, Lord, so help me to keep it simple, remembering that You are working in me both to will and to do for Your pleasure.

No Fear in Love

*There is no fear in love. But perfect love drives
out fear, because fear has to do with punishment.
The one who fears is not made perfect in love.*

1 JOHN 4:18 NIV

Lord, I thank You that Your great love conquers fear! I can love people freely because You live in me. It doesn't have to be scary to reveal my inner self. I don't have to fear rejection. I may be accepted or not, but either way I can love with confidence because Your perfect love drives out fear. Give me the courage to live that life of love.

For the Sick

*Is anyone among you sick? Let them call the elders of the
church to pray over them and anoint them with oil in the
name of the Lord. And the prayer offered in faith will make
the sick person well; the Lord will raise them up. If they have
sinned, they will be forgiven. Therefore confess your sins to
each other and pray for each other so that you may be healed.
The prayer of a righteous person is powerful and effective.*

JAMES 5:14–16 NIV

Lord, I am praying for a person who is sick right now. She needs your healing touch on her body and her emotions. Heal her pain, Lord. Help her to sense Your presence, to know You are near. Be her comfort. I ask that she would not be afraid or lonely. I pray in faith, in the name and power of Jesus, to heal my friend. I ask that You would make her well.

Serving the Lord

Whatever you do, do your work heartily, as for the Lord rather than for men, knowing that from the Lord you will receive the reward of the inheritance. It is the Lord Christ whom you serve.

COLOSSIANS 3:23–24 NASB

Some days, Lord, I feel as if I am working to please others and not You. But that's not what it is all about. It is You I am serving, only You. You give me the power to do Your will. It is from You that I receive my reward for a job well done. Thank You, God, for giving me the opportunity to serve You and You alone!

For Those in Grief

Blessed are those who mourn, for they will be comforted.

MATTHEW 5:4 NIV

Lord, my friend has deep pain in her soul. I ask that You would comfort her. Be near, Lord. Be near. May she rest in the strong and loving arms of the one who loves her most. Heal her heartache, heal her sorrow. You are acquainted with grief so You know her pain. Help her to know that You can relate and that You care. One day soon, may she find healing and wholeness again.

Missions

*Then it seemed good to the apostles and the
elders, with the whole church, to choose men from
among them and send them to Antioch.*

Acts 15:22 esv

I don't know if I could serve in a foreign country, Lord, but there are others who will and do. God, bless them. Give them strength and protection in these perilous days. Speak to their hearts. Specifically, I pray for [your church's missionary's names]. Make their message clear. Aid them in their journey. Open the hearts of those around them who dwell in darkness. Spread Your light among the nations, O God.

Light in My Darkness

Lord, often I am afraid. In the dark, challenging times of my life, I can't always see the way. I don't know what to do or where to go. But You are light! I thank You that You can see in the dark—the darkness is as light to You—so I don't have to be afraid. When my enemies try to ruin my life, they don't stand a chance, Lord. You save me. No matter what happens, I will be confident in You.

God Strengthens You

"So do not fear, for I am with you; do not be dismayed,
for I am your God. I will strengthen you and help you;
I will uphold you with my righteous right hand."

Isaiah 41:10 NIV

Lord, I need Your strength in me. Stronger than steel, Your character is so solid. I don't have to be afraid. You are with me—and that means everything. I can have joy because of Your joy in me. With Your righteous right hand, you help me, deliver me, and uphold me. As You take my hand and say, "Do not fear, I will help you," I smile in gratitude and thanks.

God's Power to Conquer Fear

Lord, You never give in to defeat. You are a strong conqueror of sin and evil. I need Your authority and influence to muscle fear out of my life. You called Moses to lead the Israelites from slavery to freedom. Lead me from my own personal bondage to walk in freedom and peace. Show Your power in my life, and let Your name be lifted up. You get the credit, Lord—let everyone know what You have done to change me.

Servants on Fire

Fan into flame the gift of God, which is in you.
2 TIMOTHY 1:6 NIV

Give me the passion, Lord, to serve You with the gifts You have given me. Reignite the enthusiasm I felt when I first began to serve You. Help me to forget about myself and to see only You. Help me to feel Your presence within me. Set me on fire for You and You alone!

Making Prayer a Priority

God, I am reaching out to You from the deepest places in my heart. I love You and want to make prayer a favorite part of my day. Help me to be consistent in spending time with You. Teach me to recognize and reject the distractions and the unending list of things that keep me too busy for You. My relationship with You is my highest priority and strongest commitment. Remind me of that, and give me the determination to spend time in prayer no matter what situations arise. Let nothing keep me from You!

Ministers

If you have the gift of speaking, preach God's message. If you have the gift of helping others, do it with the strength that God supplies. Everything should be done in a way that will bring honor to God because of Jesus Christ, who is glorious and powerful forever. Amen.

1 PETER 4:11 CEV

I bring before You this morning the minister of my church. Give him strength as he comforts, counsels, and consoles the sheep of his flock. Help him as he prepares the sermon for this Sunday, meets with the church leaders, and goes throughout his week. Protect him from the evil that surrounds him. Fill him with Your light, anoint him with Your Spirit, and give him the Word his people need to hear.

Jesus Completes His Work

"Father, the hour has come. Glorify your Son, that your Son may glorify you. For you granted him authority over all people that he might give eternal life to all those you have given him. Now this is eternal life: that they know you, the only true God, and Jesus Christ, whom you have sent. I have brought you glory on earth by finishing the work you gave me to do" (John 17:1–4 NIV).

Biblical Perspective on Money

*Now it is required that those who have been
given a trust must prove faithful.*

1 Corinthians 4:2 niv

Lord, I am thankful for the financial resources with which You have blessed me. I want to be a good steward, a wise manager, of the resources You have entrusted to me. Help me to save and spend with discernment and give to others in need. Help me to find balance—not be a hoarder or an out-of-control spender. Give me a godly view of money and how to use it in ways that will honor You.

Every Minute Counts

What I do today affects my tomorrow. Lord, help me to be conscious of time-wasters. I don't want to be idle and lazy. Show me Your plan and the things I need to put my hands to, but at the same time help me to balance my life so I take good care of my body and mind with the right amount of rest. As I walk with You, I know I am pursuing the things You want me to do. I ask You to help me be in the right place at the right time, every time.

Honoring God

For God bought you with a high price.
So you must honor God with your body.

1 CORINTHIANS 6:20 NLT

Remind me, Lord, that my service to You is a way to honor You with my body. You have done so much for me that it is overwhelming at times. Allow me to use my gift to bring greater glory to Your name so that others will be drawn ever closer to You.

Knowing What's Important

Father, help me to know what is most important. I know that growing in my relationship with You is first, so I need Your help in staying true to that commitment. Second, I need Your help in valuing the relationships You bring into my life and caring for them with the power of Your love. Please tap me on the shoulder and remind me when I'm becoming too busy. I don't want to miss the most important priorities in life.

One Body

We are members one of another.

EPHESIANS 4:25 KJV

When one of us is suffering, Lord, we all hurt. Some of my church are grieving, some are burned out, some are of ill health and unsound mind, and some are in financial distress. Lord, bless the people who make up the body of my church. Give them love and comfort. Make this body a unified body, strengthened by Your Spirit and Your love, gathered to meet in Your presence, formed to do Your will.

Everything Comes from God

Wealth and honor come from you; you are the ruler of all things. In your hands are strength and power to exalt and give strength to all. Now, our God, we give you thanks, and praise your glorious name. But who am I, and who are my people, that we should be able to give as generously as this? Everything comes from you, and we have given you only what comes from your hand (1 Chronicles 29:12–14 NIV).

Spending Wisely

For the love of money is a root of all kinds of evil.
Some people, eager for money, have wandered from the
faith and pierced themselves with many griefs.

1 TIMOTHY 6:10 NIV

Lord, You are the one who gives wisdom—and I ask that you would give me the discernment I need to spend money sensibly. I need money to pay my bills and meet my obligations. I know from Your Word that money itself is not evil; it's the love of money—greed—that makes us wander from the faith. Help me to spend the money You provide not in self-indulgence but in good judgment.

Working to His Honor

Everything I do and everything I have is for Your honor and Your glory—not mine! I am the ambassador of Your one and only Son, Jesus Christ. Give me that attitude today so that everyone who looks at me, hears me, and speaks to me will see His face and feel His presence. I want to become less so that He can become more. I am Your servant, Lord; help me to serve productively and creatively. All, Lord, to Your honor!

The Healing Edge

People. . .begged him to let the sick just touch the edge of his cloak, and all who touched it were healed.

MATTHEW 14:35–36 NIV

Lord, when I connect with You, when my body is filled with Your power and love, nothing can harm me. I am healed from within. Fill me now with Your presence. Heal my body, soul, and spirit. I praise Your name, for You are the one who heals me, saves me, loves me! Thank You for giving me life!

Great Expectations

Lord, I want to be like David, serving my own generation by Your will. No matter how small the job or role, fill me with great expectations that You are going to do a powerful work through me. I ask this not for my glory but to demonstrate to others the power of living in You. Imbue me with hope and thanksgiving. I do not know the entire plan You have for my life. Help me not to look too far ahead and thus miss the joy of day-to-day living. Thank You for hearing this prayer.

Saving and Investing

*The wise store up choice food and
olive oil, but fools gulp theirs down.*

Lord, I pray that You would lead me to wise financial advice. When I
look, help me find a trusted source who can give me direction as to
where to best save and invest my resources. Please provide for my
needs today and help me save for the future. Help me be responsible
with my finances as I trust You as my Provider.

Servant-Style Leadership

Lord, teach me to be a leader by being a servant. Your ways are so
unlike the ways of the world. Strange as it may seem, You say that
"whoever wants to become great among you must be your servant."
Help me to be more like Christ, as He did not come to be served
but to serve. Remove pride, selfishness, and arrogance from my life,
and supply me, Lord, with humility and a heart that serves.

Strength in Weakness

*Therefore I take pleasure in infirmities, in reproaches,
in needs, in persecutions, in distresses, for Christ's
sake. For when I am weak, then I am strong.*

2 CORINTHIANS 12:10 NKJV

It's a paradox, but it is Your truth. When I am weak, I am strong because Your strength is made perfect in my weakness. Because You are in my life, I can rest in You. With Your loving arms around me, I am buoyed in spirit, soul, and body. When I am with You, there is peace and comfort.

Mission Field

Jesus, teach me, lead me, and send me. I realize the mission field is right outside my front door. My desire is to open the doors of opportunity as I find them in my community. Whether I plant, water, or harvest, my desire is to be a useful servant for You. Show me what needs to be done, and strengthen my resolve to do Your will enthusiastically.